# *ALL THINGS*
# *CHRISTMAS*
## *The History & Traditions*
## *of Advent and Christmas*

**Books by E. G. Lewis**

**The Seeds of Christianity™ Series**

*WITNESS* — Book One
*DISCIPLE* — Book Two
*APOSTLE* — Book Three
*MARTYR* — Book Four

**Commercial Fiction**
*PROMISES*

*LOST*

**NonFiction**
*At Table with the Lord* - Foods of the First Century
*All Things Christmas*— *The History & Traditions of Advent and Christmas*
*In Three Days* - The History & Traditions of Lent and Easter

## The Rome Series
Book One— Everyday Life in the Roman Empire
Book Two— Games, Sports, and Entertainment

## Reviewers praise *All Things Christmas*—

"A great read over coffee and cookies as you look forward to the Christmas holidays. This would make a wonderful hostess gift for those having parties as well as a thoughtful gift for friends and family."

"Not only does he describe the origins of Christmas well, but he also gives insightful information on many famous and inspiring people of the Bible such as Jesus, Jesus' mother, Mary, Joseph and others."

"E.G. Lewis does a great job exploring the history behind many of our most popular Christmas traditions and giving us ideas to incorporate little-known ancient traditions into our modern celebration."

"A lovely, fun, and helpful book that can especially help parents explain the symbolic and spiritual meaning of why we do what we do at Christmas. It helps to draw the focus back to the 'reason for the season' and provides meaningful ideas on how to celebrate our Savior's birth."

"A wonderful book to read, anytime!"

— ∞⊂≫ —

Cover: *The Nativity of Jesus* by Gerard vanHonthorst, 1622

1. Nonfiction: Christian—Historical    2. Nonfiction: Christian— Biblical    3. Nonfiction: History of Christmas

# ALL THINGS CHRISTMAS

## The History & Traditions of Advent and Christmas

By

**E. G. Lewis**

**Cape Arago Press**
P.O. Box 771
North Bend, OR 97459
www.capearagopress.com

# TABLE OF CONTENTS

## — BONUS CHAPTERS —

## INTRODUCTION

Welcome to this study of All Things Christmas — The History & Traditions of Advent and Christmas. Following the flow of Seasons in the Church year, the annual rhythm of Feasts and Fasts has become a sacred journey that has sanctified the lives of many Christians for at least fifteen centuries.

For those unfamiliar with the term, Advent (coming from the Latin word *adventus* meaning arrival or coming) is a liturgical season observed in many Christian churches as a time of expectant waiting and preparation for the celebration of the Nativity of Jesus. The season encompasses the four Sundays prior to Christmas and can be as short as 22 days or as long as 28 days.

Even though we've celebrated Christmas all our lives, there is still much to be learned about the lore, legend and reality of what is arguably most people's favorite holiday. Surprisingly enough, this holiday — which has been so stereotyped and commercialized — was not even celebrated by the very earliest Christians. Each year we hear the plea to return Christmas to its religious roots by putting Christ back into Christmas. Though most everyone agrees that to do so would be a good thing, no one seems to know how to go about accomplishing the task. Our suggestion would be to focus on the one part of the equation which remains under our control and concentrate on what happens within your own home.

The Latin word *adventus* carries with it a particular implication of waiting for the arrival or coming of someone or something having great importance. Today, this season of Advent is observed by many Churches and denominations. Both the Roman and Eastern Orthodox branches of Catholicism, along with its lesser branches such as the Coptic, Melkite, Armenian and Syrian Churches celebrate it, as well as the Anglican, Lutheran, Presbyterian and Methodist denominations of Protestantism.

### A Little Lent

The very earliest celebrations of Advent, beginning in the

fourth century, involved some form of fasting. Advent begins the Church's liturgical year and fasting is the traditional whole-body response to life's sacred moments. As the season of spiritual preparation for Christ's coming, Advent began as a time to prepare oneself for the great feast to come — the Christmas celebration of Jesus' birth that follows in the church year. In this way Advent is a counterpart to Lent, the season when Christians traditionally fasted in preparation for the celebration of Easter.

Because Advent falls in the tenth month (*December* in Latin meaning *the tenth month*), early Christians associated it with the fasts proscribed in Zechariah 8:19. Traditionally, the Advent fast focused on abstaining from certain foods for a period of time as a physical and spiritual act that nourishes prayer. And these traditions are indeed ancient. In his letter, *On the Fast of the Tenth Month*, Pope Leo the Great (d. 461) reminded believers that the Advent fast was instituted so that "when all the ingathering of the crops was complete, we might dedicate to God our reasonable service of abstinence, and each might remember so to use his abundance as to be more abstinent in himself and more open-handed towards the poor."

Though the Advent fast was eliminated in the Western Church in the 1960's by the changes of Vatican II, it remains alive and well in the Eastern Churches. Orthodox Christians generally fast from meats, dairy, oil, and wine during Advent in order to identify with the simple fare that Adam and Eve shared before their sin, when God supplied their nutrition in the Garden of Eden without the consumption of animals.

Fasting helps us proclaim God's story, a story of love requiring watchful preparation of our hearts and minds, and patient waiting for God's faithful completion of his divine promises. Advent can be seen as a pilgrimage to encounter Christ similar to accompanying our fellow citizens to greet a royal delegation outside the city and journey back home with the noble personage. In our Advent preparation we go with fellow disciples to welcome our coming king.

Unfortunately, the prevailing trend is toward a secular

holiday season running from Thanksgiving to New Year's Day — a festival of consumption. This approach distracts us from the true meaning of these seasons. The wisdom of the Church is simple: the gravity of Christ's Incarnation beckons us to feast and rejoice, but only after a period of preparation that includes fasting.

There remains a tension between Advent and Christmas, in which one entails sacrifice and waiting while the other demands full-fledged celebration. Keeping that in mind, we have tried to focus on many of the spiritual aspects of the season while including family projects and recipes whenever it seems appropriate. Hopefully, these and the rest of the book will enhance many Christmases to come.

The final segment contains a multi-chapter excerpt from the first book in the Seeds of Christianity™ Series. The story follows the life of Rivkah, a young Jewish girl who accompanies her father to the stable in Bethlehem on that first Christmas and holds the newborn Jesus. It follows her continuing interaction with Mary, Joseph and the infant Jesus until the family flees to Egypt. We hope you and your family enjoy this brief glimpse into these Biblical events and life in the First Century.

## *Chapter Two*
## Advent Wreathes and Calendars

Over the years the celebration of Christmas and the onslaught of commercialism directed at us from every side has nearly overwhelmed Advent. As Christmas begins to draw near, many parents look for a way, or ways, to prepare the children of the household for the big day and, in the process, direct these young minds toward the spiritual underpinnings of the holiday rather than its more commercial aspects. While there are many things parents can do to accomplish this, two of the most common approaches are the Advent Wreath and/or an Advent Calendar.

### The Roots of the Advent Wreath

With a history dating back to the Middle Ages, the Advent Wreath is steeped in symbolism. It has four candles, one for each of the four Sundays before Christmas. A fifth white candle is often added in the center of the circle and burned during the twelve-day Christmas season. Many stores sell pre-made wreathes along with a set of candles. For the more adventurous, it can be an easy do-it-yourself project.

The wreath itself can be as simple or elaborate as desired. Some people use circles of Styrofoam, or florist's oasis, as the underpinnings of their wreath. Wreathes can just as easily be made using a square of plywood with holes drilled at each corner or candle holders attached at those positions and in the center if desired. Once the wreath's frame is covered in greenery, it assumes a round shape regardless of its base.

The traditional colors for the Advent candles are three purple and one rose. Because of its long association with royalty, purple candles symbolize the coming of the Prince of Peace. The single rose candle is lit during the third week of Advent beginning with *Gaudete* Sunday (from the Latin word for rejoice) to celebrate having reached the half-way point of the season. Some Protestant churches prefer to use four red candles, reflecting their use in Christmas decorations, along with a white one at the center.

The wreath is covered with various evergreens, each having its own symbolism. The laurel signifies victory over persecution and suffering; pine, holly, and yew signify immortality; and cedar, strength and healing. Holly also has a special Christian symbolism. Its prickly leaves serve as a reminder of the crown of thorns. The circular shape of the wreath, which has no beginning or end, symbolizes the eternity of God, the immortality of the soul, and the everlasting life found in Christ. Children may want to add pine cones, nuts, or seed pods to decorate the wreath as symbols of life and resurrection.

**The Domestic Church**

The earliest altars centered around the open fire of the hearth. Here a family elder...a grandfather perhaps...led the rituals and blessings of daily life. Even as religious practices became organized around the Temple with its priests, the home retained its important spiritual place of prayer and worship. Early Christianity confirmed this tradition. In the earliest centuries communal worship occurred in the homes of the faithful. Over time the home's centrality in worship declined, replaced by special buildings designed for group worship such as Churches and Cathedrals.

Yet there is still a place in our lives for the domestic church, a special spot, a holy gathering place for family prayer. With its candles and central position at the table, for a few weeks the Advent Wreath naturally lends itself to that purpose. The following are a suggested, though not required, series of prayers to be used with the Wreath. Each night you may want to accompany them with a short Bible reading. Many families find the first passages of Luke work especially well. Beginning with Zechariah and Elizabeth, Luke tells the story of the Angel Gabriel appearing to Mary, Caesar Augustus' census, and culminates in the birth of the Christ Child.

**Suggested Advent Wreath Prayers**

On the First Sunday of Advent, a parent blesses the wreath, saying: "O God, by whose word all things are sanctified, pour forth Thy blessing upon this wreath, and grant that we who use it may prepare our hearts for the coming of Christ and receive from Thee abundant graces. Amen."

Each day of the first week of Advent, the youngest child lights one purple candle and the family prays: "O Lord, stir up Thy might, we beg thee, and come, that by Thy protection we may deserve to be rescued from the threatening dangers of our sins. Amen."

During the second week of Advent, the oldest child lights the purple candle from the first week plus a second purple candle and the family prays. "O Lord, stir up our hearts that we may prepare for Thy only begotten Son, that through His coming we may be made worthy to serve Thee with pure minds. Amen."

During the third week of Advent, the mother (or another child) lights the two previously lit purple candles plus the rose candle and the family prays, "O Lord, we beg Thee, incline Thy ear to our prayers and enlighten the darkness of our minds by the grace of Thy visitation. Amen."

During the fourth week of Advent, the father (or another child) lights all of the candles of the wreath and the family prays,

"O Lord, stir up Thy power, we pray Thee, and come; and with great might help us, that with the help of Thy grace, Thy merciful forgiveness may hasten what our sins impede. Amen."

For the twelve days of Christmas, light the center white candle and pray, "God of love, Father of all, the darkness that covered the earth has given way to the bright dawn of your Word made flesh. Make us a people of this light. Make us faithful to your Word that we may bring your life to the waiting world. Amen." Continuing the readings after Christmas up to Luke 2:40 completes the birth narrative. You may also want to go to Matthew's account of the Magi.

**The Advent Calendar**

The Advent Calendar is a more modern innovation that many families enjoy. Like the wreath, the calendar can be as plain as a series of numbered squares of paper or cloth hung in the shape of a Christmas tree, or as fancy as wooden cabinets or houses with doors and drawers for each day. Part of the Advent Calendar's popularity lies in its versatility. It can be structured to convey a religious message for the Christmas season, or take a more secular approach.

In either case, the calendar counts down to Christmas as the children turn over a tag, open a little door, or reach into a pocket to discover a small hidden treasure. Stores sell inexpensive cardboard calendars with paper doors that open to reveal a picture.

Some people insert candies in the pockets or drawers, while others put in small nativity figurines. Each day another figurine is removed from that day's pocket, door, box or envelope, etc. One day a lamb or an angel is revealed; on another day it might be a shepherd or a Wise Man. This continues right up to the day before Christmas, or Christmas day itself.

Felt figures can also be used and pinned to an adjoining board. The solid figures can become ornaments to be hung on the tree or used to assemble a separate nativity scene in a small crèche. A corresponding portion of the Christmas story can be read for each day's nativity figurine until it is completed on the last day with the baby Jesus.

**Cloth Calendar with Pockets**

One of the most important parts of parenting is creating memories. If used properly, both the Advent Wreath and/or an Advent Calendar will create family traditions and happy memories for your children that can last a lifetime.

## *Chapter Three*
## THE FOODS of ADVENT

The Advent season presents an inherent conflict. Since Advent, like Lent, was a time of preparation and fasting it became the custom to practice some sort of abstinence...perhaps giving up a favorite food as a sober reminder of the season. However, Advent anticipates Christmas and cannot help but be suffused with joy as well. Traditional treats — especially on St. Nicholas Day, December 6, and during the Golden Nights, December 16 to 24 — have long been a part of the Advent observance. In parts of Europe, especially Germany and Scandinavia, a number of traditional snacks and goodies have come to be associated with the Advent season. Here are a few that you may wish to try.

### Cinnamon-Spiced, Sugared Walnuts & Pecans

This is a super easy and quick way to make a sweet and nutty treat for your family or guests.

### Ingredients:
3 C walnut halves
1 ½ C pecan halves
2 C sugar
1 C water
¼ tsp. of cinnamon

**Preparation:**

In a heavy skillet, dissolve the sugar in the water and add the nuts. Cook and stir until the water disappears and the nuts have a sugary appearance. Remove from heat. Pour nuts onto a baking sheet and quickly separate, using two forks. Cool and serve.

## *DIPLES*

Pronounced, *Thee-ples*, they get their name from the Greek word for fold. This Greek recipe for a folded, deep-fried dessert is an Advent favorite that is said to memorialize the swaddling clothes of the infant Jesus.

**Ingredients:**
3 eggs
¼ C sugar
2 C all-purpose flour
1 Tbsp. oil (to oil hands)
Oil for frying

**Syrup:**
1 C honey
1 C sugar
3/4 Tbsp. orange juice
½ C water
½ cinnamon stick
2 cloves

**Preparation:**

Whisk the eggs vigorously until pale. Add sugar and

continue whisking until the sugar is dissolved. Slowly add the flour, whisking constantly until a dough forms. Oil your hands and knead the dough until smooth. Wrap in plastic wrap and rest for 30 minutes.

Divide the dough in half. Roll each half until very thin or use a pasta machine. To test if it is thin enough, when you lift a corner of the dough and gently blow under it, it should lift. Cut the dough into 4" wide strips and divide into 3" sections.

Heat the oil in a large frying pan to a depth of about 2 ½ inches. Hold one edge of the dough with tongs and place in the hot oil. As they start to puff, roll into a cylinder shape using another pair of tongs or a long carving fork. Drain on absorbent paper.

Place syrup ingredients in a large saucepan and cook over low heat until hot. Dip the *diples* into the hot syrup, making sure they are completely coated then drain and cool. Serve decorated with ground walnuts and almonds dusted with cinnamon.

**Spicy Chocolate Almonds**

These almonds are typically found prior and through the Christmas season in Germany. The process is an easy one; coat the nuts with spices, bake and then dip in chocolate. This recipe yields about one cup of chocolate covered nuts. It can be proportionally increased as desired.

**Ingredients:**

½ to 1 C powdered sugar, divided

4 tsp. butter or margarine, divided

1 tsp. apple or pumpkin pie spice

1 to 1½ C raw almonds

I C semi-sweet chocolate baking chips

**Preparation:**

Combine 1/4 c. powdered sugar and the spice mix. Coat the raw almonds with the powdered sugar mixture by tossing together in a bowl or placing both in a plastic bag and shaking. Lay the almonds out in a single layer on a cookie sheet and bake at 325 degrees for about 15 minutes, or until almonds are fragrant and toasted a bit. Remove from oven and cool to lukewarm.

Place chocolate chips and butter in a microwave-safe bowl and heat by 20 second increments, stirring in-between, until smooth.

Place the warm almonds in the chocolate and stir to coat. Remove with a pair of forks and drop them singly back onto the baking sheet covered with waxed paper. Separate as needed. Cool the almonds (place in refrigerator, if necessary). When the chocolate has set up, remove the coated nuts from the sheet and toss them with fresh, powdered sugar to coat. Store in a cool place or in the refrigerator.

### *Speculaas* - St. Nicholas Cookies

In Holland these spicy ginger cookies are traditionally made using a St. Nicholas mold and served on the feast day of St Nicholas, December 6th. The name of these cookies is derived from the Latin word *speculum*, meaning mirror. Since the cookies were formed in a carved wooden mold, the cookie becomes a mirror image of the mold. A similar cookie can be found year round in grocery stores as Dutch Windmill Cookies.

## Ingredients:
3 C all-purpose flour
1 ½ tsp. ground cinnamon
1 tsp. ground cloves
1 tsp. ground ginger
1/8 tsp. baking powder
1/8 tsp. salt
1 C butter, softened
1 ¼ C packed brown sugar
1 egg
½ C sliced almonds

## Preparation:
In a medium-sized bowl, mix the flour with spices, baking powder and salt and set aside. In a large bowl, beat butter and sugar at high speed until light and fluffy. Beat in the egg and mix well. Stir in by hand half the flour mixture then add the remaining flour and almonds. Mix with a wooden spoon or knead with hands. Divide the dough into four parts, wrap in plastic and refrigerate for several hours. (If you are using a mold, chill it as well.)

Preheat oven to 350 degrees F and grease two cookie sheets. Remove one quarter of the dough from the refrigerator and flatten it with your hands. Oil your mold and lightly flour it. Using your fingers, press dough firmly into the mold. Trim any excess with a knife. Transfer the cookies onto greased cookie sheets with a spatula, spacing them about one inch apart. Re-refrigerate dough trimmings to be re-rolled later. Lightly flour but do not re-oil cookie mold and repeat process with remaining dough.

When the cookie sheets are full, bake for 20 - 25 minutes or until golden brown around the edges. Cool on a rack and store in a covered tin.

## *Pfeffernüsse* Cookies

These German cookies, often served at Christmas, most likely became associated with Advent because they are typically baked several weeks early. This is because the flavor of *Pfeffernüsse* deepens and sharpens with age. So if you plan to enjoy these easy-to-make cookies at Christmas, you'll want to bake them around the first week of Advent.

**Ingredients:**
1 C butter
1 C sugar
2 large eggs
½ C white corn syrup
½ C molasses
1-2 tsp. anise extract (depending upon preference)
1 teaspoon cinnamon
½ teaspoon allspice
½ teaspoon cloves
½ teaspoon nutmeg
1 teaspoon baking soda
1/3 cup warm water (from the tap, or micro-waved for a few seconds)
6½ cups flour

**Preparation:**
Preheat oven to 375 degrees F, and place rack in center of the oven.

Cream butter and sugar in a mixing bowl that is large

enough to hold all ingredients. One at a time, beat in eggs, corn syrup, molasses, anise extract and spices. Dissolve baking soda in warm water, add to mixture, and beat again. Add flour and mix until all ingredients are well incorporated. The dough should be somewhat stiff. You may wrap the dough in plastic wrap and refrigerate for half an hour or so, or continue if you're in a hurry.

Take a handful of dough and roll it into a long cylindrical sausage shape about one inch in diameter. Repeat until you've formed all the dough into cylinders. Pinch off one-inch pieces of dough from the cylinders and roll between your hands to make small balls. Place dough balls onto greased baking sheets. Bake for 10 to 12 minutes. The cookies are done when baked through and starting to brown on top. Roll cookies in powdered sugar while still warm, cool and store in an airtight container.

## Aging:

*Pfeffernüsse* will store well in airtight containers at room temperature. They will keep up to 8 weeks. *Pfeffernüsse* are quite soft when first baked, but quickly become harder. As they age they absorb moisture and soften somewhat. If you can't resist dipping into the stash, when they are in their hard stage, *Pfeffernüsse* make a particularly good dunking cookie.

### Chocolate-Dipped *Nussecken*

Nut cakes or bars are popular German bakery products. Cut on the diagonal, they are often called *Nussecken,* or nut triangles. Nuts, butter and sugar make this nut bar recipe with a butter crust very rich, so cut them small. You can bake these nut bars in an 8 x 8 or 7 x 11 inch pan, or double the recipe for a 9 x 13 inch pan.

## Ingredients:
## Crust:
5 Tbsp. butter or margarine
1/3 C sugar
1 tsp vanilla extract
1 egg
1 C plus 3 T. flour

½ tsp baking powder
½ tsp salt
2-3 T apricot jam

**Preparation:**

Cream sugar and butter, beat in egg and vanilla extract. Combine flour, baking powder and salt and add to butter mixture, making a dough. Press the dough into a greased pan. The bigger the pan, the thinner the bars. Spread the dough with apricot jam and set aside.

**Filling:**

7 Tbsp. butter
½ C sugar
1 tsp. extract
2 Tbsp. water
1 C ground hazelnuts
3/4 C chopped hazelnuts

**Preparation:**

Bring butter, sugar and water to a boil on the stove. Stir and cook for several minutes until the sugar is dissolved and the mixture is foamy. Stir in all the nuts and remove from heat. Spoon the filling over the crust and smooth. Bake in a preheated, 350 degree oven for 25 to 30 minutes, or until light brown around the edges and set in the middle. Cool completely then chill.

**Decorating:**

Cut the bars into squares then across the diagonal, making triangles. Remove the cookies to a work surface lined with waxed paper. Melt 1 C chocolate chips with 1 Tbsp. butter in the microwave at 15 second intervals, stirring after each until smooth and hot. Dip the bottoms of the nut bars into the hot chocolate and remove excess chocolate with a table knife or similar tool. (Some people also dip the edges or corners.) Place back on the parchment paper and allow the chocolate to harden. After the cookies have cooled, store them in an airtight tin between layers of wax paper. You may also freeze them.

*— Bon Appétit —*

## *Chapter Four*
## CHANUKAH, THE FESTIVAL OF LIGHT

## **A Priest Fills the Menorah with Oil**

Although the two festivals have no relationship to each other, the Jewish Festival of Chanukah and the Christian celebration of the Christmas season often overlap so it seems appropriate to include Chanukah in a study of Christmas.

In the Jewish calendar of Feasts and Festivals, Chanukah, or the festival of lights, begins on the eve of Kislev 25, and lasts eight days. It is the newest of the Jewish Feast and Festivals in that it was first celebrated in 165 BC. The date varies. For instance, Chanukah occurred between December 1st to December 9th in 2010; in 2011, December 20th to 28th; in 2012, December 8th to 16th; in 2013, November 27th to December 5th; and in 2014, December 16th to 24th.

Chanukah celebrates the triumph of light over darkness, purity over adulteration, spirituality over materiality. It memorializes events recorded in the Biblical Books, 1 & 2 Maccabees.

## The History of Chanukah

The Chanukah story begins with Alexander the Great. Following his untimely death, his Empire was divided among his generals. Ptolemy, for instance, took Egypt and most of the Holy Land. Seleucius took the adjoining area north and east of Ptolemy's which included central Anatolia, the Levant, Mesopotamia, Persia, today's Turkmenistan, Pamir and parts of Pakistan. Much of the eastern part of the empire was conquered by the Parthians under Mithridates I of Parthia in the mid-2nd century BC. Seleucid kings continued to rule from Syria until their eventual overthrow by the Roman general Pompey.

About 170 years before the birth of Christ, the Jewish nation was ruled by the Seleucid king, Antiochus IV called *Epiphanes,* meaning "Manifest of God." However, the historian Polebius gave him the epithet *Epimanes* —madman — because of his cruelty. Antiochus tried to impose his Hellenistic beliefs upon the Jews. He removed their High Priest and installed his own man, Menelaus. He then marched on Egypt. When Rome overpowered Antiochus in Egypt, a rumor spread that Antiochus was dead. The former high priest, Jason, raised an army and led the people in a rebellion, driving Menelaus out.

Enraged by his defeat, Antiochus attacked Jerusalem and restored Menelaus. He ordered his soldiers to cut down anyone they met and to slay those who took refuge in their houses. They massacred young and old, killing women, children, and infants. In the space of three days, eighty thousand were lost. Forty thousand met a violent death, and an equal number were sold into slavery.

The Second Book of Maccabees tells the story of a mother and her seven sons. Jewish legend calls her Channah. The sons were arrested and taken before the king. One-by-one, he ordered the sons to abandon their religious beliefs and one-by-one they refused and were killed. As they took the last boy away Channah told her son, "Tell your ancestor Abraham, 'You bound only one son upon an altar, but I bound seven.'"

**Channah Laments the Loss of her Seven Sons**

## The Book of Judith

The story of *Yehudit* is told in the Book of Judith which is read in every Synagogue during Chanukah. Her city came under siege by a huge Seleucid army. Rather than starve to death, the people appealed to their leader to surrender. The Jewish leader asked for five days of prayer before he decided whether or not to surrender. Meanwhile, Judith, a young widow, went to meet with the general. He invited her to dinner and she fed him her homemade cheese and wine. He got drunk and passed out. In an act reminiscent of David and Goliath, she cut off his head with his own sword, put it in her picnic basket and took it to the leader of the Jews. The soldiers panicked when they realized their general was dead and the Jews defeated his army.

## The Maccabean War

Judah was the third son of Mattathias the Hasmonean, a Jewish priest from the village of Modiin. He and his brothers led a rebellion against the Seleucids. He was a great general and defeated Antiochus's armies time and again though often greatly outnumbered. For this reason people began to call him Judas Maccabeus, or *Judah the Hammer*. When the war was over, he and his family ruled the country for the next 100 years. His descendents are often referred to as the *Maccabees* or the *Hasmoneans*.

Once the Maccabees were victorious, the Jews set about to purify the Temple that the Hellenists had defiled. When they entered the Temple, however, they could find only one jug of oil with the high priest's seal of purity still intact. Worse yet, there was only enough oil in the jug to last for a single day. Regardless, they used it to light the menorah and this one day's worth of oil miraculously burned for the full eight days of the purification. This miracle has been celebrated ever since as the Festival of Light, or Chanukah.

## Special Chanukah Celebrations

Chanukah commemorates an oil-based miracle, which explains why Jews eat oily foods to commemorate it. Some eat fried potato pancakes known as *latkes*, while others eat *sufganiyot*, deep-fried doughnuts. It is also customary to eat cheese since one of the greatest victories resulted from Judith feeding the enemy cheese.

During Chanukah it is also customary to give *gelt* (money) to children, so they can be taught the value of charity. During the Hellenistic oppression, the Greeks outlawed Torah schools, so the children had to study in the forests. They posted a sentry to alert them of patrols, and when the alert came, the children would hide their texts and start playing with *dreidels* (spinning tops).

By playing with a *dreidel* during Chanukah, children commemorate the courage of those heroic children. A driedel, by the way, is a four-sided top with the letters *nun* נ, *gimmel* ג, *hay* ה, and *shin* ש carved on its sides, which stand for the words *nes gadol hayah sham* — A great miracle happened here.

Each day of Chanukah Jews recite the complete *Hallel* in their morning prayer service. They also insert a special prayer of thanksgiving, *V'al Hanissim*, in the prayers and Grace after Meals. Every morning they read from the Torah about the inauguration offerings brought for the dedication of the Tabernacle — reminiscent of the Maccabean re-dedication.

## Chapter Six

### *Laganum Fructus* – An Ancient Fruitcake

Fruitcakes are traditionally served during the Christmas season and so we decided to whip up an ancient fruitcake as a yuletide treat. It's called *Laganum Fructus*, which is Latin for *Cake of Fruit* or *Cake with Fruit*. Fruitcake was quite popular with the soldiers of Rome's Legions. It was aged with wine and the alcohol preserved the cake, preventing spoilage. Consequently, a Legionnaire could pack his *laganum fructus* into his *loculus*, a traveling pack or duffel bag, and count on the cake keeping until he finished snacking on it.

This recipe calls for some aging, so it's best to make it well ahead of when you plan to serve it. Now let's get something straight. It doesn't matter whether you love fruitcake or hate the thought of the stuff; gather the kids together and bake one anyway. It's a good way to make the Biblical era real to your children. We gathered a Christian Education Class together and had a fruitcake making demonstration.

There are two distinct styles of fruitcakes, very cakey or very fruity. The recipe provided in this book definitely leans to the fruity side of things. That is, it's a lot of fruit held together with a little bit of dough. The ancient recipe for this fruitcake consisted of four primary ingredients: pomegranate seeds, pine nuts, dried fruits, and barley flour. The first hurdle you'll encounter is how to soften pomegranate seeds to the point where they can be chewed without the risk of breaking a tooth. An easy way to circumvent this is to substitute pomegranate juice, and that's what our recipe calls for.

Most of the pine nuts sold in the grocery stores are imported from China and are very often bitter. The best pine nuts are harvested in the mountainous regions of Nevada and New Mexico. They aren't in stores, but can be ordered direct over the Internet. If you're a stickler for authenticity, by all means order some. They make wonderful eating. However, they are harvested in the Fall and typically aren't ready for shipment until

Thanksgiving or later...although you can pre-order. They also sell out pretty quickly, so don't delay.

A cheaper alternative would be to substitute slivered almonds. This is a legal replacement since almonds were available in that part of the world in the 1st Century. In addition to eating the nuts out of hand and cooking and baking with them, they also pressed the nuts for their oil and made almond milk, which they used for cooking.

**Ingredient list** along with comments:

1 C olive oil

1 C honey

1 C pomegranate juice

4 eggs

2 C barley flour

1 C wheat flour...if you want to be authentic use whole wheat flour

2 tsp salt

2 tsp ground cinnamon

1 tsp nutmeg

1 tsp baking powder...This is an easy, but illegal ingredient. The only leavening available in the 1st Century was natural yeast. They would have mixed some of their starter into the barley flour.

1 C of pine nuts

1 ½ C raisins

1 ½ C chopped dates

3 C mixed dried fruit...Equal amounts of apples, plums (prunes), and apricots works well.

Citron was the only citrus known in ancient Israel so it is a legal ingredient. If desired, you may add some diced, candied citron. Adjust the quantities of the other fruits proportionally.

**Optional**: Rose water, wine, grape or apple juice for basting.

**Aged Fruitcake Sliced for Serving**

**Directions**: Heat oven to 275 degrees. Grease two 8 1/2" x 4 1/2" loaf pans and line them with parchment or wax paper. Sift all dry ingredients together and set aside. Dice the fruit small, mix in a bowl and set aside. Combine oil, eggs, pomegranate juice and honey. Alternately add portions of the dry ingredients and the oil mixture to the fruit, mixing well each time.

When batter is complete, pour it into the prepared pans and bake for 2 ½ to 3 hours. Begin checking for doneness with a toothpick after 2 ¼ hours. Let stand 15 minutes before removing from pans. Do not remove the paper. When thoroughly cooled, carefully remove paper and wrap the loaf in cheesecloth soaked with any of the basting ingredients. Enclose in plastic wrap and then in foil and store in the back of the refrigerator for 2 weeks.

### The Final Analysis

We took our show on the road and prepared *Laganum Fructus* for the youngsters in a Christian Education Class. This was done as a teaching tool, a way for the these young people to experience a reasonable facsimile of what people may have eaten 2,000 years ago. Obviously, our goal was to make something that tasted good, but we felt accuracy should trump tasty.

To be brutally honest, the cakes were okay, but hardly great tasting. The cake is heavy on *dark* fruit...raisins, dates, and prunes and, for the sake of authenticity, we used whole wheat and barley flour. The combination of these two factors yielded a dark cake with a strong, but not particularly sweet flavor. Part of the problem is that our modern pallet is accustomed to a much higher level of sweetness than the ancient one. What tasted sweet and good to them seemed coarse and dry to us. We served the cake with Cool Whip so the children could supplement the taste a bit.

This in no way means the experiment/demonstration was a failure. Whether the cake was of blue ribbon quality or not, it was a success because we replicated something that they would never have otherwise experienced. I encourage you to pursue this recipe with the same goal in mind.

## *Chapter Six*
## Caesar Augustus' Census

**Arriving in Crowded Bethlehem**

"In those days a decree went out from Caesar Augustus that all the world should be enrolled. This was the first enrollment, when Quirinius was governor of Syria. And all went to be enrolled, each to his own city." —Luke 2:1 – 3

The older translations (KJV and Douay-Rheims) identify the Roman official in charge as *Cyrenius,* while the newer translations call him *Quirinius.* The older versions simply used the Greek form of his name, whereas the newer ones use the Latin. Either way, the opening of Luke's birth narrative contains a passage that critics of the Gospel's historicity have criticized. Some claim that there was no census, others that Publius

Sulpicius Quirinius was never Governor of the Roman Provence of Syria, still others say it doesn't align with historical records. Let's start at the beginning and work our way through these, and other, objections.

**Why Bother With a Census in the First Place?**

The Constitution of the Unite States requires a national census every ten years. The reason for this is that under the stipulated two-house Legislature, the number of Congressional Representatives for each state is proportional to its population. Anticipating the growth and expansion of the original thirteen colonies, the Founding Fathers realized that over time changes in population density would occur necessitating a re-adjustment of the seats in Congress. Following a census, the individual states redraw their congressional districts adding or subtracting as necessary and adjusting to population shifts within the states' boundaries.

The Roman Empire, however, was a dictatorship. Though certain lower-level positions were subject to election, they had no need to re-district and re-adjust as we do today. The driving force behind the Roman census would have been economic rather than political. Like all governments, Rome depended on tax revenue for its survival.

Early on, Rome developed a practice known as tax farming. Under this system, an individual or group of individuals formed a corporation and bid for the tax revenues of a particular region. This accomplished several things. It transferred the work and worry of collecting the taxes to another party. It also guaranteed a given level of revenues. Thus, Roman officials knew with certainty how much would come from a particular Provence and could budget accordingly. Meanwhile these tax corporations subdivided and resold regional taxing rights which were subdivided again and again down to the local administrator who actually collected the money. As it moved back upstream, each succeeding level skimmed a little off and passed the rest up the ladder not unlike the Mafia.

Regardless of how the taxes were applied or what was being

taxed, then as now the money ultimately came from the pockets of individuals. And, the more individuals, the more revenue that could be collected. So those at the top of the pyramid wanted an accurate count of the population so they could estimate future income. Caesar Augustus was no slouch in this department. In his *Lives of the Caesars*, Roman Historian, Seutonius, reports that Augustus, "...revived the office of the Censor which had long been disused and whose duty it had formerly been to take an account of the number of people." During his 44-year reign, Augustus took three censuses...only slightly less frequently than the United States does.

### Trying to Date Luke's Census

To date the census Luke is speaking of, we first must examine the text. The key phrase is, "This was the first enrollment, when Quirinius was governor of Syria." Luke used the Greek word *protos*, meaning foremost (in time, place, order or importance) — before, beginning, best, chief, first (of all), or former. Unfortunately, the early translators of the New Testament didn't concern themselves with the possibility of a historical conflict posed by their use of the word *first*. If they had, the passage might have read something like, "This was the census before the one taken while Quirinius was governor of Syria." This would have eliminated any confusion as to which census he was speaking of.

### Caesar Augustus' tax of 6 AD

The Roman Historian, Dio Cassius, writes that Caesar Augustus decreed a census for purposes of taxation for all the inhabited earth, essentially the Roman Empire, in 6 AD. By 5 AD the military expenditures for the Roman legions had exceeded available income, and "Augustus lacked funds for all these troops." (Dio Cassius, Roman History LV 24:9) To overcome this deficit, Augustus "established the tax of 5%, on the inheritances and bequests which should be left by people at their death to any except very near relatives or very poor persons." Dio Cassius claims to have found references to this tax set down in Caesar's memoranda.

It was, in fact, "a method which had been introduced once

before, but had been abolished later, and was now revived. In this way, then, he increased the revenues." (Roman History LV 25:5-6) Establishment and collection of such a tax would require a census to register transferable assets, such as land, and to record genealogies to establish who was and was not "a very near relative."

Josephus, in his Antiquities, notes the response to this decree in Judea, "Now Cyrenius, a Roman senator, and one who had gone through other magistracies, and had passed through them till he had been consul, and one who, on other accounts, was of great dignity, came at this time into Syria, with a few others, being sent by Caesar to be a judge of that nation, and to take an account of their substance. Coponius also, a man of the equestrian order, was sent together with him, to have the supreme power over the Jews. Moreover, Cyrenius came himself into Judea, which was now added to the province of Syria, to take an account of their substance, and to dispose of Archelaus' money; but the Jews, although at the beginning they took the report of a taxation heinously, yet did they leave off any further opposition to it." (Ant. XVIII 1:1)

We should point out here that the *Archelaus* Josephus mentions is Herod Archelaus, the son of Herod the Great, and recently deposed ethnarch of Judea. Augustus named Herod Archelaus ruler of Samaria, Judea, and Idumea following his father's death. He ruled from 4 BC until 6 AD when Augustus removed him because of incompetence. So in the Jewish homeland the census served a two-fold purpose. First, it fulfilled the edict of Caesar Augustus and facilitated his new tax. Secondly, it closed the books on Archelaus' administration before the territory was annexed to the Provence of Syria and Coponius took office as the regions first Prefect.

Archelaus appears in Matthew's Gospel in Chapter 2:20-23 where he is cited as the reason Joseph chose to go to Nazareth rather than return to Judea where they had lived prior to the flight into Egypt. "'Rise, take the child and his mother, and go to the land of Israel, for those who sought the child's life are dead. And he rose and took the child and his mother, and went to the land of Israel. But when he heard that Archelaus reigned over Judea in place of his father Herod, he was afraid to go there, and being warned in a dream he withdrew to the district of Galilee. And he went and dwelt in a city called Nazareth, that what was spoken by the prophets might be fulfilled, 'He shall be called a Nazarene.'"

But the census of 6 AD can't be the one Luke is referring to. Since it was specifically designated for the military, the Roman troops would have conducted the census. There would have been no going "to be enrolled, each to his own city."

## Going Back to Ancient Writers

Recall that Dio Cassius tells us that this was the second attempt at a military tax and that it had been introduced once before, but later abolished and was now being revived. There was only one prior tax designated specifically for the military, and this must be the decree Luke referred to. The decree for taxation combined with a census at the time of Jesus' birth was likely that first unsuccessful attempt to support the military treasury.

However, because there's no record of when the first tax was imposed, it can't be dated with certainty. But we can find mention of it by other early writers. Tertullian (155-245), the Christian theologian, notes that a census in Judea took place under Sentius Saturninus, who served from 9-6 BC. He writes, "But there is historical proof that at this very time there were censuses that had been taken in Judea by Sentius Saturninus, which might have satisfied their inquiry respecting the family and descent of Christ." (Against Marcion IV:19)

## Revisiting the Gospel of Luke

It's very plausible that Luke's intent was to say that the enrollment at the time of Jesus' birth was the first one, as distinguished from the later one when Quirinius was governor of Syria. Quirinius, by the way, was appointed Governor of Syria in 6 AD and was in office during the second census to complete the transition from Archelaus to Coponius. The Greek can be interpreted to say: "This census was first one, which came before the one Quirinius held while governor of Syria," which validates the historicity of Scripture.

And finally, one must reconcile the seeming contradiction that Luke describes the Jewish method of returning to one's tribal headquarters to be counted when the Romans typically counted people where they were. The key difference is that this census was to establish inheritance taxes and people would have to go back to tribal region regardless of who was conducting the count. As a descendant of David, and thereby of the tribe of Judah, Joseph had to go back to town where the necessary land records and genealogies were located.

It is known that a significant number of Judeans relocated to Galilee in the latter years of the First Century BC. The fact that after the visit of the Angel Gabriel, Mary "arose and went with haste into the hill country, to a city of Judah, and she entered the house of Zechariah and greeted Elizabeth," (Luke 1:39-40) provides further support for the notion that both Mary and Joseph had familial ties to Judea.

## Putting it all together

So let's quickly sum up. We know that Quirinius was Governor of Syria from 6 AD to 9 AD and supervised a census while Governor. We also know that another, earlier tax and census was imposed sometime before he became Governor. We know Herod the Great was still alive when Jesus was born. We know this from Matthew who, in reference to the Wise Men, tells us, "And being warned in a dream not to return to Herod..." (Matt 2:12) And secondly because Luke tells us in the opening of his Gospel, "In the days of Herod, king of Judea, there was a priest named Zechariah..." (Luke 1:5)

Most experts date Herod's death as occurring in 4 BC. For instance, Josephus states that Herod's son, Philip the Tetrarch's death took place after a 37-year reign, in the 20th year of Tiberius...i.e. 34AD. If his father died in 4 BC, Phillip would have taken office in 3 AD. Consequently, we can say with good certainty that the first tax/census Luke mentions, and Jesus' birth, must have occurred prior to or very early in 4 BC.

## *Chapter Seven*

# WHY IS CHRISTMAS ON DECEMBER 25<sup>TH</sup>?

Ask a dozen people, "Why is Christmas on December 25<sup>th</sup>?" and you're likely to end up with a variety of answers none of which is, "Well, because that's the day Jesus was born."

The skeptics in the group will agree that Christ was definitely NOT born on December 25<sup>th</sup>. You've heard their justifications. After all, everyone *knows* religion is nothing but myth and superstition, a single story told and retold around the world according to mythologist Joseph Campbell in his book *The Hero with a Thousand Faces.*

**Differing Ideas**

As the Church grew and came into its own, according to the prevailing consensus, it began adapting and assimilating left and right. No matter where these early Church Fathers went, the first thing they did was incorporate the local pagan beliefs and holidays into Christianity. After all, how else could they make their message appeal to the masses? So Christmas has nothing to do with Jesus. It was derived from the solstice traditions of the ancient Babylonians...or was it the Assyrians? No, maybe it was the Persians or the Medes, the Greeks...the Romans, the

Egyptians, the Norse, the Celts, the Druids, the...the... And on and on it goes. It seems the only ones who haven't been credited with originating Christmas are the Mayans and the Aztecs. And, given enough time, they may still make it to the big leagues.

## Importance of Solstices and Equinoxes

There's one thing that needs to be understood. Nearly all early cultures had strong traditions built around the solstices and equinoxes. They had to. There was no such thing as Greenwich Mean Time for them and calendars were ephemeral things. Day length varied from long to short and back again. Driven by the moon and months, the festivals associated with them could move around if not carefully watched.

Meanwhile, critical factors such as the correct time to plant had to be known with certainty. Without phone, fax, or email, and saddled with a calendar that demanded constant tinkering, the only dependable measure of time lay in the heavens. Even the American Indians carefully tracked the solstices. It allowed them to predict the migration patterns of game animals, attend pre-arranged councils, and meet at specific times and places to trade with other tribes.

Should anyone be surprised that most ancient cultures had winter festivals of one sort or another? No, the greater surprise would be if they didn't. But if the early Christians didn't piggyback their Feast Days onto someone else's, how in the world did they arrive at a suitable date?

## Searching for Clues

The Bible offers few clues. Celebrations of Jesus' Nativity are not mentioned in the Gospels or in Acts and the date of his birth is not given, not even the time of year. The biblical reference to shepherds tending their flocks at night when they hear the news of Jesus' birth (Luke 2:8) might suggest the spring lambing season. Yet we have to be cautious when extracting precise meanings from what is generally a theological narrative.

This is also a good place to point out that references to cold and snow in Christmas Carols such as *The First Noel*, "On a cold winter's night that was so deep..." or *Still, Still, Still*, "One can hear the falling snow..." are the result of moving an event which occurred in the Middle East to the less temperate climes of Northern Europe.

In reality, the first Christians cared little about when Jesus was born. There is no mention of birth celebrations in the writings of the Christian Fathers such as Irenaeus or Tertullian. Origen of Alexandria even mocks the Roman celebration of birthdays, calling them *pagan practices*. Everything seems to indicate that Jesus' birth was not even celebrated by the Early Christian believers; their focus remained squarely on, as Paul said, "Christ crucified."

The earliest writings, Paul and Mark, make no mention of Jesus' birth. Only the Gospels of Matthew and Luke provide accounts of the event; although, unlike the Passion narrative, neither attempts to anchor it in time. Further details of Jesus' childhood don't appear until the Second Century in apocryphal writings such as the *Infancy Gospel of Thomas* and the *Proto-Gospel of James*. And, though they provide the names of Jesus' grandparents and details of his education, they ignore the issue of his birth date.

## Accounting for the Date

Perhaps there is a different, and better, way to account for the origins of Christmas on December 25th — the Jewish tradition that creation and redemption should occur at the same time of year. The Babylonian Talmud preserves a dispute between two early Second Century rabbis who share this view, but disagreed on the date. Rabbi Eliezer states, "In Nisan the world was created; in Nisan the Patriarchs were born; on Passover Isaac was born...and in Nisan they (the Patriarchs) will be redeemed in time to come." The other rabbi, Joshua, dates these same events to the following month, Tishri.

## Establishing the Date of the Nativity

Could it be that the dates of Christmas and Epiphany may well have resulted from Christian theological reflection on such chronologies? Could Jesus have been conceived on the same date he died, and thus born nine months later?

Around 200 AD Tertullian reported his calculation that the 14th of Nisan, the day of the crucifixion according to the Gospel of John, equated to March 25th in the Roman (solar) calendar. March 25th, which comes nine months before December 25th, was later recognized as the Feast of the Annunciation, the commemoration of Jesus' conception. If the ancient Christians believed that Jesus was conceived and crucified on the same day of the year, then the logical thing to do would be to establish his day of birth exactly nine months later...on December 25th.

This idea appears in an anonymous Christian treatise titled *On Solstices and Equinoxes*, which comes from fourth-century North Africa. It states, "Therefore our Lord was conceived on the eighth of the *kalends* of April in the month of March (March 25th), which is the day of the passion of the Lord and of his conception. For on that day he was conceived and on the same he suffered."

Augustine, too, was familiar with this idea. In *On the Trinity* he wrote, "For he is believed to have been conceived on the 25th of March, upon which day also he suffered; so the womb of the Virgin, in which he was conceived, where no one of mortals was begotten, corresponds to the new grave in which he was buried, wherein was never a man laid, neither before him nor since. But he was born, according to tradition, upon December the 25th."

**The Eastern Church**

If you remain skeptical, consider one final point. The Eastern Church also links the dates of Jesus' conception and his death. However, instead of working from the 14th of Nisan in the Hebrew calendar, Orthodox scholars used the 14th of the first spring month (Artemisios) in their local Greek calendar, which corresponds to April 6th. April 6th is, of course, precisely nine months before January 6th, the date on which the Eastern Church celebrates Christmas.

There is evidence that April was associated with Jesus' conception and crucifixion in the East. Bishop Epiphanius of Salamis writes that on April 6th, "The lamb was shut up in the spotless womb of the holy virgin, he who took away and takes away in perpetual sacrifice the sins of the world." Even today, the Armenian Church celebrates the Annunciation in early April (on the 7th, rather than the 6th) and Christmas on January 6th.

Here we have Christians in two parts of the world both calculating Jesus' birth on the basis that his death and conception took place on the same day (March 25th or April 6th) and coming up with two close but different results for his birth (December 25th and January 6th). Connecting Jesus' conception and death in this way may seem odd to modern readers, but it reflects the ancient belief of the whole of salvation being bound up together.

This begs the question, what about all those stories of Christmas being adapted from pagan holidays? In cases such as this it's sometimes helpful to ask yourself, "Who benefits from such a theory?" Clearly such ideas bolster those who seek to disprove Christianity's claims about Jesus and the saving grace He offers mankind. One might even go so far as to say that the ultimate beneficiary of such a claim would be the Evil One, the Father of Lies, the Prince of Darkness, in short, the Satan.

Interestingly enough, the first suggestion that Jesus' birth celebration was deliberately set to coincide with the time of pagan feasts didn't surface until the 12th Century. A marginal note on a manuscript of the writings of the Syriac biblical commentator Dionysius bar-Salibi states that in ancient times the Christmas holiday might have been shifted from January 6th to December 25th so that it fell on the same date as the pagan *Sol Invictus* holiday. In the 18th and 19th centuries, Bible scholars developed the study of comparative religions and picked up on this idea. They claimed that because the early Christians didn't know when Jesus was born, they simply assimilated the pagan solstice festival for their own purposes, claiming it as the time of the Messiah's birth and celebrating it accordingly.

Don't you believe it.

### *Chapter Eight*

### SAINT NICHOLAS versus SANTA CLAUS

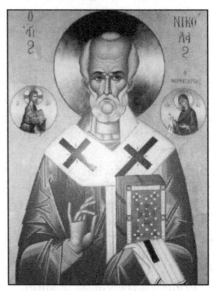

### An Icon of St. Nicholas

Saint Nicholas versus Santa Claus? Hmmm, sounds a bit like a promo for an upcoming event on the Wrestling Channel, doesn't it? Let's take a closer look...

Bursting with excitement, the announcer says, "Welcome Ladies and Gentlemen. You've tuned into the smack-down of the century, a match made in heaven. At the end of this evening only one man will remain standing. Who will it be?"

The announcer continues as the camera focuses on a slim wrestler in gold trunks as he stretches and tests the ropes. The white robe he's wearing has a gold crown on the back. "Here we have the perennial champion...St. Nick. They used to call him *Jolly old St Nick*, but we haven't seen that famous grin of his lately. With his popularity tanking I guess he doesn't have much to smile about. Even the church ladies have sworn off Nick. Times change and today's favorite can be tomorrow's has been. I can't help wondering if he's bitten off more than he can chew tonight. Could this be the match that forces him into permanent retirement?"

Loud cheers and shouts interrupt the announcer. The sound of people stamping their feet reverberates throughout the arena. The camera quickly pans to the opposite corner of the ring where an overweight man in a red spandex suit, mask and cape is climbing through the ropes.

The announcer must shout to be heard over the crowd. "There he is, folks. This is what the crowd's been waiting for...the man who thinks he can unseat Old Nick. The crowd is going crazy. Listen, they're chanting his name. In all my years I've never seen anyone as wildly popular as Mr. C. They say he flew in from up north especially for this match. This Mr. C is more than just a wrestler; he's a juggernaut...an overwhelming force."

The retired wrestler who provides color commentary leans close to the mike. "Sure he's popular, but we know nothing about this Mr. C character. I mean, it's like he's been created out of thin air by the media. Who, or what, is hiding underneath that mask and red suit?"

The announcer shakes his head and smiles. "He's a man of mystery, all right. No one knows anything about him, but for some unexplainable reason they love him anyway."

The bell rings and the two men step forward to meet with the referee at the center of the ring.

**The Real Saint Nicholas**

St. Nicholas was born in 271 and died around 342 or 343 near the town of Myra in what was called Asia Minor, present day Turkey. At the time of his death, Nicholas served as Bishop of Myra. The story of how he achieved that office is an interesting one. During the last official Christian persecution by the Roman Empire, the bishops from the surrounding cities and villages were called together to choose a successor when the Bishop of Myra died.

Nicholas made it a habit to rise early and go to church to pray. That morning an elderly priest greeted him when he entered the sanctuary. "Who are you, my son?"

"Nicholas the sinner," the young priest replied, "and I am your servant."

"Come with me," the old priest said.

Nicholas followed him into a room where the bishops had assembled. The elderly priest addressed the gathering. "I had a vision that the first one to enter the church in the morning should be the new Bishop of Myra. Here is that man, Nicholas."

Nicholas ended up leading his congregation through the worst, and last, official Roman persecution of the Church. Diocletian had been Emperor for 19 years when he began a widespread persecution of Christians in the year 303. Diocletian left office two years later, but his successor, Galerius, continued the harassment.

Nicholas was exiled and imprisoned during this period and only returned to his diocese in 311 when the Edict of Toleration ended the persecution. Two years later in 313 Constantine's Edict of Milan made Christianity a legal religion. Nicholas is also said to have participated in the Council of Nicaea in 325, although his name is not listed among the attendees.

## Known for His Charitable Acts

Nicholas was a friend to the poor and helpless while serving as Bishop. Following the admonition of Christ that "when you give alms, do not let your left hand know what your right hand is doing, so that your alms may be in secret;..." (Matthew 6:3), he moved about the city aiding the poor and needy without anyone knowing it.

The story is told of three young girls whose father couldn't afford their dowry and so they weren't able to marry. Nicholas tossed a bag of coins down their chimney so that they would have the necessary dowry without knowing where it came from. By coincidence the girls had hung their stockings from the mantel to dry and Nicholas's sack ended up in one of the stockings. This legend led to children in many European countries leaving their shoes on the hearth or hanging stockings on the mantle on the eve of St. Nicholas' Feast Day, December 6th.

In addition to aiding children in need or distress, Nicholas is also said to have rescued innocent men who were falsely imprisoned. He became known as the friend and protector of all in trouble or need. He was said to have been able to calm raging seas and rescue sailors in peril, causing his fame to spread throughout the Mediterranean area.

Centuries after his death, his remains were transported by sailors to Bari, a port in Italy. A monument was constructed over his grave and the town became a destination for those pilgrims intent on honoring him. His fame eventually spread around to the Atlantic Coast of Europe and the North Sea making St. Nicholas day part of the European Christmas holiday tradition. The Protestant Reformation of the 16th Century slowed, but never completely eradicated St. Nicholas traditions and observances of his comings and goings.

## Coming to America

He traveled to America with Dutch colonists who settled in New York and called him *Sinterklaas*. In 1809 American author, Washington Irving, took the first step that eventually morphed the saintly Bishop into the blatant marketing tool known as Santa Claus. Irving's satirical *Knickerbocker's History of New York* made frequent reference to a jolly St. Nicholas-type character who was an elfin Dutch burgher with a clay pipe.

More damage was done in 1823 when a poem called, *A Visit from St. Nicholas*, was published. Better known by its first line, *Twas the Night before Christmas*, it tells the story of a man who awakens to noises outside his home and sees St. Nicholas arrive in a sleigh pulled by eight reindeer...all with names. Interestingly, the stockings had been hung by the chimney with care in the hopes that St. Nicholas would soon be there...not on December 6th, but on December 25th! He was dressed all in fur, no doubt to protect him from wind chill while flying about in an open sleigh. His eyes how they twinkled, his dimples how merry...His cheeks were like roses, his nose like a cherry. His droll little mouth was drawn up like a bow, and the beard of his chin was as white as the snow. He was chubby and plump, a right jolly pipe-smoking old elf.

## Thomas Nast's Image of St Nicholas

During the Civil War, political cartoonist Thomas Nast did a series of drawings for Harper's Weekly magazine based on the descriptions found in the poem and Washington Irving's work. For the first time, Santa moved into the arena of public opinion by letting it be known that he supported the Union cause. Nast continued drawing Santas until 1886. More than St. Nicholas' appearance changed during the 20 odd years that Nast did his drawings. His name, which had been the Dutch *Sinterklaas* or German *Sankt Niklaus,* changed into the Americanized phonetic approximation, Santa Claus.

It didn't take long for this new Santa Claus to become decidedly commercial. Dozens of artists competed with each other producing Santas in a wide variety of sizes and shapes. By the 1920s the standard American Santa had emerged. A rotund, normal-sized man, instead of an elf, he had a flowing white beard, wore a fur-trimmed red suit, and though seldom seen with his pipe, continued to travel from his North Pole residence in a sleigh pulled by reindeer.

In short order this new Santa became a shameless shill. He

willingly hustled any and all products no matter how silly or mundane. If you want Marilyn Monroe, James Dean or Elvis Presley in your ad, even though they're dead, it'll cost you an arm and a leg. Mickey Mouse and Donald Duck aren't even real people, but you'll still have to pay the Disney Studios a royalty for them. Meanwhile Santa Claus, who retains just enough of a saintly persona to make him marketable, comes free of charge.

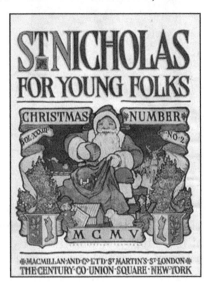

Devoid of scruples and free for the taking, Santa Claus became the ultimate pitchman. Not even a saint can compete with that, as if St. Nicholas cares. The latest word is he's decided to give up the wrestling circuit and enjoy a leisurely retirement spent occasionally visiting churches or answering prayers when and if he's invited to do so.

## *Chapter Nine*
## A TALE OF TWO MOTHERS

**Elizabeth Greets Mary**

"It was the best of times, it was the worst of times, it was the age of wisdom, it was the age of foolishness, it was the epoch of belief, it was the epoch of incredulity, it was the season of Light, it was the season of Darkness, it was the spring of hope, it was the winter of despair, we had everything before us, we had nothing before us..."

Rather than *A Tale of Two Cities*, this is A Tale of Two Mothers — Hannah of the Old Testament and Mary of the New Testament. Interestingly enough, the words Charles Dickens wrote about the French Revolution describe the circumstances of these earlier times quite well.

Hannah lived at a time of uncertainty and transition. The children of Abraham left Egypt and wandered in the desert forty years before Joshua led them into the Promised Land. There they established themselves as a nation, a nation ruled not by Kings, but by Judges. Now, after 350 or more years of life under Judges, the Israelites had begun growing restive. They look around and see Kings at the head of every other nation and say, "Give us a king to govern us."

Mary, a virgin in Nazareth betrothed to a man named Joseph, lived a thousand years after Hannah. But she, too, lived in an era of uncertainty and transition. The remnant had come back from Babylon and rebuilt their nation only to see it fall under the control of the Seleucids. A revolt by the Maccabees established an independent Jewish nation for a time, but now the Romans and their client king, Herod, ruled the Jews. Despite these dire circumstances a feeling of expectancy bubbled beneath the surface, animating the nation. The time in Daniel's prophecy of the 70 weeks was nearing fulfillment; the day of restoration would soon be at hand.

## Appointing a King for the Jews

It was the Judge Samuel who anointed Saul the first King of the Jews and later, when Saul faltered, he anointed a young shepherd boy, David, to replace him. Clearly Samuel had a special place in God's plan for Israel. Samuel, son of Hannah, instituted great changes that affected the lives of all Jews.

We meet Elka'nah and his two wives, Penin'nah and Hannah in 1 Samuel. Penin'nah had borne him many children and Hannah had none. Consequently, when they went to Shiloh Elka'nah gave Penin'nah many portions to make offerings for herself and all her children. Hannah, meanwhile, got only a single portion. To add to Hannah's pain, Penin'nah ridiculed her because of her inability to conceive.

Desperate, Hannah offers the Lord a deal: Give me a son and I will give him back to you for all the days of his life, and no razor shall touch his head. (A reference to the Nazarite vow.) Eli the priest promises the Lord will answer her prayer. Sure enough, Hannah's prayer *is* answered and she names the boy Samuel — *I have asked him of the Lord.*

When Samuel is weaned, she takes him to the Temple as promised and gives him to Eli to raise and mentor. It is at this point, 2 Samuel 2:1, that we hear her prayer of praise and thanksgiving to the Lord.

**Hannah Prepares Samuel for the Temple**

### HANNAH'S SONG

My heart exults in the Lord; my strength is exalted in the Lord. My mouth derides my enemies, because I rejoice in thy salvation.

There is none holy like the Lord, there is none besides thee; there is no rock like our God.

Talk no more so very proudly, let not arrogance come from your mouth; for the Lord is a God of knowledge, and by him actions are weighed.

The bows of the mighty are broken, but the feeble gird on strength.

Those who were full have hired themselves out for bread, but those who were hungry have ceased to hunger. The barren has borne seven, but she who has many children is forlorn.

The Lord kills and brings to life; he brings down to Sheol and raises up.

The Lord makes poor and makes rich; he brings low, he also exalts.

He raises up the poor from the dust; he lifts the needy from the ash heap, to make them sit with princes and inherit a seat of honor. For the pillars of the earth are the Lord's, and on them he has set the world.

He will guard the feet of his faithful ones; but the wicked shall be cut off in darkness; for not by might shall a man prevail.

The adversaries of the Lord shall be broken to pieces; against them he will thunder in heaven. The Lord will judge the ends of the earth; he will give strength to his king, and exalt the power of his anointed.

## A Second Young Woman

We first encounter Mary at prayer in her Nazareth home. (Luke 1:26) The angel Gabriel appears to her and tells her she is to become the mother of the Messiah. Afterwards, Mary travels to Judah where she visits her cousin, Elizabeth, who is also pregnant.

Elizabeth greets her with the cry, "Blessed are you among women, and blessed is the fruit of your womb!" She goes on to say, "And blessed is she who believed that there would be a fulfillment of what was spoken to her from the Lord."

Mary responds with what has come to be known as the *Magnificat*...the opening word of the prayer in its Latin version.

### MARY'S SONG

My soul magnifies the Lord, and my spirit rejoices in God my Savior, for he has regarded the low estate of his handmaiden.

For behold, henceforth all generations will call me blessed; for he who is mighty has done great things for me, and holy is his name.

And his mercy is on those who fear him from generation to generation.

He has shown strength with his arm, he has scattered the proud in the imagination of their hearts,

He has put down the mighty from their thrones, and exalted those of low degree; he has filled the hungry with good things, and the rich he has sent empty away.

He has helped his servant Israel, in remembrance of his mercy, as he spoke to our fathers, to Abraham and to his posterity forever.

## Comparing the Two Women

Types and archetypes are found throughout the Bible. People and events in the Old Testament find their counterpart in the New Testament. The life of Christ is particularly rich with such comparisons. Throughout his Epistles, Paul develops corollaries between Jesus and various events and figures from the Old Testament. Jesus is *the new Adam,* the *Paschal Lamb,* we are all members in the *Body of Christ,* and on and on. Though longer, the parallels between Hannah's Song and Mary's are impossible to miss. The tone, the imagery, her references to the poor and down-trodden...they're all there.

Nestled within the stories surrounding these two women are many other interesting points and counterpoints. Yet on closer inspection we begin to see that while there is congruence between Hannah's Song and Mary's, Samuel is not an archetype for Jesus, but for John the Baptist. For instance, Hannah was unable to conceive. Elizabeth, too, had reached an advanced age and never had a child. We are told before he is born that Elizabeth's son, John, will take the Nazarite vow just as Hannah promised Samuel would before his birth. Since Samuel was given to the Lord and raised by Eli, one might say his *father* was a priest. John's father, Zechariah, was also a priest.

The Hebrew word *Mashiach* means *the Anointed One.* Samuel, as Judge, identified and then anointed David to become king of Israel. It is David who is the archetype for Jesus, and like Samuel, John identified Jesus and anointed him through baptism.

In retrospect we find that what began as a tale of two women expands to become a tale of three women, their sons, and the leaders these sons anointed.

## Chapter Ten

# IN THE FULLNESS OF TIME

"But when the fullness of time had come, God sent forth his Son, born of woman..." — Galatians 4:4

Jesus last words to his disciples were, "Go therefore and make disciples of all nations..." On examination, it appears God chose the perfect time to send his Son into this world so that the Apostles could disperse this new faith, which would come to be called Christianity, throughout the world. How and why did He choose that particular moment in history?

### A Moment in Time

The phrase the fullness of time is ripe with expectancy... waiting...longing. It brings to mind a convict in his cell leaning against the barred window and wistfully watching the sun set. Another day is done, one less day to be served. Perhaps that was what Paul had in mind when he penned those words. A captive world bound and chained by sin anxiously awaiting its promised Redeemer. Clearly this is how the Jews felt as they struggled under the thumb of Rome and Herod.

Though most people ascribe the Book of Daniel to the period of the Babylonian Exile (586-536 BC), there are some who would have us believe it to be much newer than that. They say it was composed during the Maccabean period, more precisely in the time of Antiochus IV, Epiphanes (175-164 BC). However, the date of the Book of Daniel is not relevant to this discussion. We know that Jesus made a specific reference to a passage from Daniel in Matthew 24:15 when he said, "So when you see the desolating sacrilege spoken of by the prophet Daniel, standing in the holy place..." This validates both the Book and its existence in the First Century.

We also know that apocalyptic literature of all kinds was very popular during that period of time. As much as anything it was probably a backlash to high taxes and oppressive rulers. The Messianic hope reached a fever pitch in the early 1st Century. Several sections of the Book of Daniel contain Messianic predictions. The primary one being the prophecy of the seventy weeks found in Daniel 9:24-27.

### Deciphering Daniel's Prophecy

Like all prophetic writings, as specific as it sounds, the prophecy of the seventy weeks still required interpretation. When did one begin counting the weeks? What was to occur when this period of time had elapsed? Some would say it would mark the arrival of the Messiah, but in what form? Would that be the date of his birth, the beginning of his ministry/revolt, the declaration of his kingdom? Things were just obscure enough to allow for multiple opinions. Consequently, a number of Messianic Pretenders arose around the time of the birth of Christ. Their appearance, and almost instant success in gathering a conquering army, was no doubt motivated as much by frustration as by prophecy.

Messiahs aside, there were other factors that had to be in place and, in retrospect; we can see the hand of God moving the various playing pieces into position. Astronomers have developed a set of criteria necessary for a planet to support life. Without factors such as a temperate climate, oxygen, liquid water and so on, life as we know it, whether created or evolved, can never exist. Perhaps it would be helpful to draw up a similar list of factors required for any Messianic movement to grow and flourish. First of all, the people had to be open to the message. While readiness may be hard to quantify, we can make several observations.

## Putting the Pieces in Place

Though the presumption among Jews was that the Messiah would be a warrior king, the message Jesus brought was spiritual, not temporal. This meant that there had to be a certain level of intellectual curiosity, if you will, about spiritual matters. The First Century was a time of wildly divergent religious beliefs. As the Romans annexed territory, they also assimilated the local gods of that region into their pantheon of divinities. This combined with a general freedom of worship meant that a person could explore any and all alternatives.

Plato and Aristotle developed the idea of a soul, or spiritual essence, that was immortal. The rise of philosophies such as Hedonism, Epicureanism, and Stoicism, which generally rejected the established gods, created a spiritual void while the mystery cults emphasized a savior-god and required worshipers to offer blood sacrifices, making the gospel of Christ which involved a single ultimate sacrifice acceptable.

## An In-Gathering of the Jews

All the spiritual hunger in the world won't do you much good if your core group is dispersed and inaccessible. The Jews went through a general in-gathering in the years preceding the birth of Christ. The existence of the Temple in Jerusalem and the requirement that all adult males return to celebrate the Pilgrim festivals of Pesach, Shavuot and Sukkoth meant that those believers who were geographically distant could still keep up with the latest happenings and newest ideas. The passage in Acts 2:9 relating to Pentecost lists sixteen different nationalities, or language groups, present in the city for the Festival. The miracle of Pentecost is, of course, that all who heard Peter speak understood him. Having heard, these people could carry this message (gossip) back to where they'd come from.

## The Unity of the Roman Empire

It would be difficult, if not impossible, to disperse a message across an area consisting of competing kingdoms, city states, petty fiefdoms and territories ruled by war lords and tribal chieftains. This is the primary reason the Roman Empire stalled in its conquest of northern Europe. These are the conditions the Romans encountered as they moved into areas such as Ireland, Scotland, and Germany...areas they never completely subdued.

The Germanic tribes, in fact, inflicted the greatest military defeat Rome ever experienced when they slaughtered three Roman Legions plus six cohorts of auxiliaries and three squadrons of cavalry in the Battle of Teutoburg Forest. Hadrian built his famous wall from the North Sea to the Irish Sea in an attempt to stop incursions by the Picts of Northern Scotland.

Despite its problems in the outer reaches of the Empire, Rome unified and civilized a huge area that stretched from northern Africa and the Middle East, around the Mediterranean Basin into the Balkans and across the greater part of Europe. Reciprocal trade relationships connected the Roman Empire with India, China and great portions of the African continent. A single governmental authority meant that travelers could move across the Empire and beyond freely. Such freedom to travel would have been impossible in prior eras.

The Roman Empire, inherited a culture left behind by the Greeks. Most of the Empire was multi-lingual, speaking two if not three languages. While the affairs of the Empire were conducted in Latin and the average person in the Holy Land spoke Aramaic, Greek served as a common unifying language facilitating trade and commerce. Apostles carrying the message of Christianity were easily able to communicate regardless of the locale they found themselves in.

## Roman Roads and Bridges

As the Roman Empire grew, the necessity to rapidly move troops from one area to another became a priority. Rome attacked the problem by constructing a network of highways throughout the land. Upon conquering an area one of the first things the Romans did was build forts along the perimeter and link them with all-weather roads of stone block over a base of gravel. Rome recruited its army from the provinces and shifted the men from one region to another. It made good sense not to conscript an army from your former enemies and then go home and leave them in charge, much better to have Britons in Gaul, Macedonians in Syria and so on. As Rome shifted troops, they also disseminated cultural and religious beliefs. The earliest introduction of the gospel to Britannia was the result of the efforts of Christian soldiers stationed there.

It has been said that everyone participates in God's plan, some willingly and some unknowingly. Given man's limited scope, most of the time we find it impossible to see the good that God extracts from evil. It is difficult, if not impossible, to imagine anything worthwhile coming from the regimes of Hitler, Stalin, Mao Tse-Tung, Pol Pot, Idi Amin, et al. And yet, the same thing can be said for Caligula, Nero, Domitian or Diocletian. Even with a 2,000 year perspective it's still difficult to make sense of the actions of such despots.

And yet God, with his eternal perspective and omniscient power, can arrange the affairs of this chaotic world in such way as to accomplish his goals...in the fullness of time.

## *Chapter Eleven*

## THREE VIEWS of SAINT JOSEPH

Though we know little about him, St. Joseph, the husband of Mary and foster-father of Jesus, played a critical role in the Holy Family. Most of our information concerning St. Joseph comes from the birth narratives in the Gospels of Matthew and Luke. There are also several apocryphal accounts and legends regarding both Joseph and Mary that may, or may not, provide further illumination.

### The Finer Details

Both Matthew 13:55 and Mark 6:3 refer to Joseph as a *tekton*, a craftsman. Tradition has settled on his craft being wood working, thereby making him a carpenter. Whether he performed general work such as making yokes for oxen, plows and so on, worked mainly in the construction trade, or did fine woodwork such as carvings and finish details can never be known.

We also know Joseph was a man of humble means since he presented the sacrifice of two turtledoves or a pair of pigeons when he took Jesus to the Temple for Mary's purification. An offering of birds was the standard for those who could not afford a lamb. We know too that he was a holy and observant Jew since the Gospel refers to him as "*a righteous man.*"

## Did Jesus have Brothers and Sisters?

Matthew 13:53-56 says, "And when Jesus had finished these parables, he went away from there, and coming to his own country he taught them in their synagogue, so that they were astonished, and said, "Where did this man get this wisdom and these mighty works? Is not this the carpenter's son? Is not his mother called Mary? And are not his brothers James and Joseph and Simon and Judas? And are not all his sisters with us? Where then did this man get all this?"

The question would appear to have been settled then and there. However, that is not the case. The three major divisions of Christianity have each developed their own viewpoint on this question. And each of them revolves around Mary as much as Joseph.

## The Protestant Viewpoint

Luther argued that correct interpretation of scripture rests not with the Church but "*in the heart of the pious believer.*" This has led the majority of Protestants to follow the practice of *plain or explicit* interpretation of the Bible. This rule says that when the plain interpretation of Scripture makes common sense, seek no other; take every word at its primary, ordinary, usual, and literal meaning unless the facts of the immediate context, studied in the light of related passages and fundamental truths indicates otherwise.

At first glance, this passage from Matthew appears to be exactly such a situation. However, it comes with certain suppositions, making it problematic. Mary and Joseph are now assumed to be the parents of at least six additional children after the virginal and miraculous conception of Jesus. This assumes

Joseph was young enough to father this brood.

We know Jesus was the firstborn, and therefore the oldest, because they made an offering of two turtledoves or pigeons at the Temple (Luke 2:22-24) to redeem him as required by Numbers 18:15: "...nevertheless the first-born of man you shall redeem..." This becomes contradictory when one considers that Jesus assigned John with the task of caring for his mother from the cross. Why did he need to do this if he had four younger half-brothers? Tradition says John moved Mary from Jerusalem to Ephesus to protect her from harm. Wouldn't her children have been upset by this and protested that she should stay with them rather than John, a non-relative?

### The Orthodox Viewpoint

Among other differences, the Eastern Church holds to a doctrine of Mary's perpetual virginity. In their traditions, Joseph was a widower with children when they married. So instead of having siblings, Jesus had older step-brothers and step-sisters.

Making Joseph an older man solves two other issues. First, if he were not searching for a wife, in the fullest sense of the word, but rather a caretaker for his children, it becomes more reasonable to view him as "a most chaste spouse"...a term the Church has applied to him from earliest times. Secondly, making him older conforms to the tradition that Joseph had died by the time Jesus began his public ministry. (The last mention of Joseph in the Bible occurs when the 12-year-old boy Jesus is left behind at the Temple and he is *not* mentioned at the wedding feast in Cana.) The Orthodox view makes Jesus the youngest child in the family. And, since he was Mary's only child, he would be solely responsible for her care when Joseph died. Were Joseph not dead, her care would have been a moot point.

### The Catholic Viewpoint

Where the Protestant view tends to a younger Joseph and the Orthodox view to an older, the Catholic view demands neither. While agreeing with the Eastern view on Mary's perpetual virginity and Joseph's death prior to Jesus' public ministry, the Catholic Church believes the Holy Family consisted of three persons: Joseph, Mary and Jesus. This, of course, necessitates charging John with her care since there was no one else.

This still leaves open the question of his "brothers" and "sisters." The Bible provides a list of these brothers. If they were not siblings, who were they? A real and close kinship between Jesus and these *brethren* is clear. But the term brethren, or brother, can be applied to step-brothers as well as to blood brothers, and in Scripture is often extended to near or even distant relatives.

Comparing John 19:25 to Matthew 27:56 and Mark 15:40, we find that Mary of Cleophas, or Clopas, was the sister of Mary the Mother of Jesus. We know she is Clopas' wife because that is the way a married woman would have been identified. So this Mary is the same Mary who was the mother of James the Less and of Joseph, or Joses. Isn't James the Lesser named in the list of apostles as the *son of Alpheus*? Yes, but it is commonly recognized that Clopas and Alpheus are different transcriptions of the same Aramaic word, *Halphai*.

## Following the Brethren Through History

We know nothing of Joses, or Joseph. Jude, however, is the author of the Epistle of Jude. He is identified *Judas Jacobi,* Jude the brother of James, in the Douay Version of Luke 6:16 and Acts 1:13. It was the Greek custom for a man to append his brother's name instead of his father's when the brother was better known. In his Epistle, Jude calls himself *the brother of James.*

Simon, like Joseph, remains a bit of a mystery. Many commentators identify him as Symeon, or Simon, who, according to Hegesippus, was a son of Clopas and succeeded James as Bishop of Jerusalem. Others have identified him as the Apostle Simon the Cananean (Matthew 10:4; Mark 3:18) or Simon the Zealot (Luke 6:15; Acts 1:13). The grouping of James, Jude (also called Thaddeus), and Simon, after the others but before Judas Iscariot, seems to indicate a connection between them.

So two, and possibly three, of these cousins were among Jesus' Apostles. This seems to be verified in 1 Corinthians 9:5

where Paul writes, "Do we not have the right to be accompanied by a wife, as the other apostles and the brothers of the Lord and Cephas?" The mention of Cephas at the end indicates that St. Paul, after speaking of the Apostles in general, calls special attention to the more prominent ones, *the brothers (brethren) of the Lord and Cephas.*

**Further Considerations**

Some would object that the brethren of the Lord couldn't have been Apostles since just months before his death they didn't believe in him (John 7:3-5). This assumption is based on a misreading of the text. They didn't doubt his powers, what they misunderstood was his Messianic mission. They wanted him to declare himself a temporal leader. This expectation remained alive among the Apostles even after his resurrection.

The final objection to the Catholic, and Orthodox, position is found in Matt 1:24-25, "When Joseph woke from sleep, he did as the angel of the Lord commanded him; he took his wife, but knew her not until she had borne a son..." It can be demonstrated from other Biblical examples that the phrase *firstborn son* neither implies other children nor does the phrase *knew her not until she had borne a son* necessarily imply that he knew her afterwards.

## Chapter Twelve
## The Birth of the *Mashiach*

"In those days a decree went out from Caesar Augustus that all the world should be enrolled...And Joseph also went up from Galilee, from the city of Nazareth, to Judea, to the City of David, which is called Bethlehem..." — Luke 2:1-4

### The Geography of Bethlehem

Bethlehem is located about five miles south of Jerusalem, on the east side of what was called the *Patriarch's Highway* that ran along the ridge between Shechem and Hebron. The city is the birthplace of one of Israel's greatest kings, David. It was in Bethlehem that David was born and raised and tended his father's sheep.

Three miles to the southeast of Bethlehem is Herodium, an elaborate retreat, residence and fortress constructed by Herod the Great. Following Herod's death, a procession of his servants, the Temple priests and his private guards, escorted his body from

Jerusalem to Herodium for burial. Ironically, Herod was buried within sight of the spot where Jesus, who he tried to kill, was born.

## Exploring Favorite Traditions

Upon research and reflection, many of the traditions surrounding the birth of Jesus are found to have little basis in fact. For instance, Jesus was most likely not born in a stable, but in the home of a member of Mary and/or Joseph's extended family in Bethlehem. This misconception arose from a mistranslation of a Greek word used in Luke's Gospel. It should have been translated as *guest room*, rather than *inn*. This familiar situation often arises when the birth narrative is presented based on Western culture rather than a Middle Eastern viewpoint. This error is easily verified by comparing Luke's use of the term *kataluma* in the Nativity story and his use of *pandocheion*, a place of public lodging, when he referred to the inn where the Samaritan brought the wounded Jewish traveler in the story of the Good Samaritan. (Luke 10:34).

Mary and Joseph would have returned to Bethlehem to register for the Roman census/tax because it was the ancestral home of their families, which traced their lineage back to David and the tribe of Judah. Although they had settled in Galilee, their tribal roots remained in Bethlehem. Recent research indicates that a group of Judeans who returned from Babylon. Following the Maccabean reclamation of the northern region s of the country, a large group of them left Judea and migrated to Galilee where they established such towns as Nazareth.

Luke also tells us that when Mary went to visit Elizabeth she "went with haste into the hill country, to a city of Judah..." (Luke 1:39).With many relatives living in and around Bethlehem, it would have been unthinkable for Mary and Joseph to seek a public inn, if one did indeed exist. In such a small village, family members would not have expected or accepted such a rejection of their hospitality especially in view of the imminent birth of Mary's first child.

There is also no indication that Jesus was born immediately after Mary and Joseph arrived, or that He was born at night. The text, "...while they were there, the days were accomplished for her to give birth," (Luke 2:6) could just as easily be interpreted to mean that His birth took place at a later time, perhaps days or even weeks after their arrival.

Most homes at the time of Christ had an interior guest room. When Joseph and Mary arrived in Bethlehem they may have found the guest room in the family member's home where they intended to stay already occupied...most likely by other relatives who had also returned to register for the census.

Arrangements would then have been made for Mary to give birth in another part of the house, presumably the family living area. Or more likely, whoever was occupying the guest room would vacate it so she could deliver her baby with complete privacy. Either way, it's safe to assume Mary gave birth to Jesus inside a family home. She also would have had a midwife in attendance along with some of her female relatives. Her extended family would never leave her alone at a time like that.

Luke most probably mentioned the availability of a manger not to emphasize any inadequacy in the conditions of Jesus' birth, but to provide a transition to the shepherds. Animals were usually brought into adjacent areas of rural homes at night for safety, and in the winter, to provide warmth. If the house was truly overcrowded, the animals could be penned outside and the area swept and cleaned. With fresh straw and a few utensils it would make an adequate overflow area. Recall how often travelers are shown bedding down in the barn in shows such as Little House on the Prairie, The Waltons, etc.

This very well may have been what happened since the angels identified the manger as the place where the shepherds would find Jesus. Mangers were typically carved from stone and measured three to four feet in length. Its cavity, cleaned and filled with fresh straw, would be just the right size and height for a baby.

Since they also mentioned the cloth wrappings used for newborns, the angels might have simply been emphasizing the normalcy of His birth circumstances rather than providing a means of identifying the baby. In any case, finding the baby lying in a manger, wrapped according to common practice, seemed to have caused no surprise to the shepherds or problems for the family members present. Jesus' birth, surrounded by loving family members, reflected the customs of a humble, First Century existence.

Jesus entered this world in conditions not uncommon to his time and much of the world today. It was not the picturesque setting that is often portrayed in the Carols and Christmas cards, but it was also not unusual or squalid conditions either.

To impose a Western interpretation on the circumstances of Jesus' birth distorts the reality of the event, the people, and the times. Jesus' birth in a local family home and his being found in a manger by shepherds is symbolic of his availability to all people, even those whom many of that era would exclude.

## *Chapter Thirteen*
## **Shepherds Keeping Watch by Night**

"And in that region there were shepherds out in the field, keeping watch over their flock by night. And an angel of the Lord appeared to them, and the glory of the Lord shone around them, and they were filled with fear." —Luke 2:8-9

### Stars of the Christmas Pageant

No Christmas program is complete without its little band of shepherds wandering across the stage or up the Church aisle. Frightened by the angel's sudden appearance, they marveled at the good news and immediately rushed to Bethlehem to see their Savior-King. As they return to their flocks, they praise God and tell all who will listen about the birth of the chosen Child.

### Digging Deeper

They finish spreading the good tidings, leave the stage, and we hardly give them another thought. But why did the announcement come to them at all? Shouldn't the angels have gone to priests at the Temple instead? Why not notify all the neighboring kings? Who were these shepherds that they should be the sole eyewitnesses of God's glory and receive history's greatest birth announcement?

## No Social Standing

Unlike the priests, in Christ's day a shepherd stood on the bottom rung of Palestinian society. They shared the same unenviable status as tax collectors and dung sweepers. Of the four evangelists, only Luke bothers to mention them.

During the time of the Patriarchs, shepherding was a noble occupation. Shepherds are mentioned early in Genesis 4:20 where Jabal is called the father of those living in tents and raising livestock. In nomadic societies, everyone —whether sheikh or slave— was a shepherd. The wealthy sons of Isaac and Jacob tended flocks (Genesis 30:29; 37:12). Jethro, the priest of Midian, employed his daughters as shepherdesses (Exodus 2:16), and eventually his son-in-law, Moses.

When the twelve tribes of Israel migrated to Egypt, they encountered a lifestyle foreign to them. The Egyptians were agriculturalists. As farmers, growers of crops, they despised shepherding because sheep and goats grazed on the crops.

## Separating the Shepherds and the Farmers

Battles between farmers and shepherds are as old as they are fierce. The first murder in history ( Cain and Abel) erupted over a farmer's resentment of a shepherd (Genesis 4:1-8). Egyptians considered sheep worthless for food and sacrifice. Egyptian art forms and historical records portray shepherds in a negative light. Neighboring Arabs, the Egyptian's enemy, were shepherds. Egyptian hatred of sheep herders climaxed when bearded Jewish shepherds gradually took over Lower Egypt.

Pharaoh's clean-shaven court looked down upon the rugged shepherd sons of Jacob. Joseph matter-of-factly informed his brothers, "Every shepherd is detestable to the Egyptians." (Genesis 46:34) Over the course of 400 years, the Egyptian prejudices rubbed off on the Israelites' and affected their attitude toward shepherding. Unbelievably, Jacob's descendants became accustomed to a settled lifestyle and forgot their nomadic roots.

When the Israelites later settled in Canaan (c. 1400 BC), the few tribes that still retained a fondness for the pastoral lifestyle chose to live in the Trans-Jordan (Numbers 32:1). After the Jews settled into their new home, shepherding ceased to hold its prominent position. As the Israelites acquired more farmland, shepherding became a menial vocation for the laboring class.

## The Angels Appear to the Shepherds

Around 1000 BC, former shepherd David emerged as king and temporarily raised the shepherd's image. The lowliness of his trade made David's promotion to the throne all the more striking (2 Samuel 7:8). While poetic sections of Scripture record positive allusions to shepherding, many scholars believe these references reflect a literary ideal, not reality.

## Prophetic Symbols

In the days of the Prophets, sheep-herders symbolized judgment and social desolation (Zephaniah 2:6). Amos contrasted his high calling as prophet with his former role as a shepherd (Amos 7:14). In general, shepherds were considered second-class citizens and unworthy of trust. Sheep herding had not just lost its appeal; it eventually forfeited its social acceptability. Some shepherds earned their poor reputations, but others became victims of a cruel stereotype. The religious leaders maligned the shepherd's good name; rabbis banned pasturing sheep and goats in Israel, except on the desert plains.

The Mishnah, Judaism's written record of the oral law, also reflects this prejudice, referring to shepherds in belittling terms. One passage describes them as incompetent; another says no one should ever feel obligated to rescue a shepherd who has fallen into a pit. Shepherds were deprived of their civil rights. They could not hold judicial offices or be admitted in court as witnesses. It was written, "To buy wool, milk or a kid from a shepherd was forbidden on the assumption that it would be stolen property."

In Jerusalem at the time of Jesus, the rabbis asked with amazement how, in view of the despicable nature of shepherds, could one explain why God was called *my shepherd* in Psalm 23.

Smug religious leaders maintained a strict caste system at the expense of shepherds and other common folk. Shepherds were officially labeled sinners, a technical term for a class of despised people. Into this social context of religious snobbery and class prejudice, Jesus stepped forth. How surprising and significant that God handpicked lowly, unpretentious shepherds to be the first to hear the joyous news that the long-awaited *Mashiach* had been born.

What an affront to the religious leaders who were so conspicuously absent from the divine mailing list. Even from birth, Christ moved among the lowly. It was the sinners, not the self-righteous, that he came to save. And, interestingly enough, though Jesus spoke of many occupations in his parables, the only job title he ever claimed for himself was that of a shepherd. Jesus said, "I am the good shepherd. The good shepherd lays down his life for the sheep" (John 10:11). Christ is also the Great Shepherd (Hebrews 13:20) and the Chief Shepherd (1 Peter 5:4). No other illustration so vividly portrays His tender care and guiding hand as that of the shepherd. Perhaps that is why he chose to have them and them alone as witnesses to his birth.

## *Chapter Fourteen*
# THE CHRISTMAS MIRACLE OF 1914

You could call it a carry-over of genteel Victorianism or view it as the all-encompassing awe that accompanies the birth of the Christ Child. Attribute it to the tug of Christmas traditions on the hearts and minds of men everywhere, if you like, or simply ascribe it to being far from home, cold, tired and lonely. Whatever its root cause, first and foremost the Christmas truce of World War I validates the commonality of all mankind.

### Keeping It in the Family

The First World War, European in origin though it eventually encompassed everyone, had a strange and unique character to it. For instance, consider the fact that the George V of England, Tsar Nicholas II of Russia and Wilhelm II of Germany were first cousins. They called each other Georgie, Nicky and Willie. How could this happen? It was a case of one thing leading to another until the interlocking mutual defense alliances of Europe toppled like a house of cards. In retrospect, it seems to resemble a Keystone Kops script more than international diplomacy.

Austria-Hungary's heir to the throne, Franz Ferdinand was assassinated in Serbia. Austia-Hungary then declared war on

Serbia, anticipating a limited engagement against its smaller neighbor. However, Serbia was an ally of Russia, so Russia began mobilizing in anticipation of aiding its ally. Germany, Austria-Hungary's ally, took this as an act of aggression and declared war on Russia. France, bound by treaty to Russia, suddenly found itself at war with Germany. And Britain, an ally of France, declared war on Germany as well. All of Britain's colonies and dominions quickly followed suit in short order. Japan, another ally of Britain, also joined the fighting. Italy managed to find a loophole in its treaty with Germany, but later entered the war on side of the Allies.

## Fighting from the Trenches

World War I was a time of trench warfare in which opposing armies both dug trenches on either side of the line of combat. The troops faced each other across this relatively narrow *no man's land* while lobbing grenades back and forth and mounting occasional assaults on each other's position. Looking back nearly a hundred years, it is easy to see that World War I had little about it to motivate the common soldier. It fit the classic definition of war being a game old men, or in this case royalty, played with young men's lives.

## The First Christmas of the War

By December, 1914 the weather was cold and wet. The trenches turned to mud and muck and were sometimes knee-deep in dirty water. Meanwhile, the war itself seemed to have reached a stalemate. As Christmas drew near various groups began agitate for a truce. A group of 101 British Suffragists composed *The Open Christmas Letter,* a public message for peace addressed "To the Women of Germany and Austria." On December 7th, 1914 Pope Benedict XV issued an appeal for an official truce between the warring parties. He asked this so "that the guns may fall silent at least upon the night the angels sang." This attempt was officially rebuffed.

The men in the field felt isolated and lonely as Christmas drew closer. The soldiers could hear their counterparts singing familiar carols in the evenings. Eventually, some of the German and British soldiers began exchanging seasonal greetings across no man's land. Soon the tension between them ebbed and the men began crossing no man's land to barter or exchange small gifts...tobacco, a sweet or other food items. Exchanging buttons from their field jackets became common.

One thing led to another and before long the men started holding carol sings and joint burial ceremonies. These friendships reached the point where no man's land was converted into a playing field where men from the opposing armies staged football games. A truce of sorts had been declared not by the leaders, but by the combatants themselves. One can't help but be reminded of that famous, "What if they held a war and nobody came?"

Though there was never an official truce, about 100,000 British and German troops were involved in unofficial cessations of fighting along the length of the Western Front. The first of these truces started on Christmas Eve, 1914, when German troops began decorating the area around their trenches in the region of Ypres, Belgium. The Germans placed Christmas trees along the rim of their trenches and added candles The British responded in kind and artillery in the region fell silent. However, the fraternization carried risks. On some occasions soldiers were shot by opposing forces. Despite these breakdowns in trust, the truce lasted through Christmas night and in some sectors even continued until New Year's Day.

**Eyewitness Accounts**

Bruce Bairnsfather, who served in the war, described it this way, "I wouldn't have missed that unique and weird Christmas Day for anything. I spotted a German officer, some sort of lieutenant I should think, and being a bit of a collector, I intimated to him that I had taken a fancy to some of his buttons. I brought out my wire clippers and, with a few deft snips, removed a couple of his buttons and put them in my pocket. I then gave him two of mine in exchange. The last thing I saw was one of my machine gunners, who was a bit of an amateur hairdresser in civilian life, cutting the unnaturally long hair of a docile Boche, who was patiently kneeling on the ground whilst the automatic clippers crept up the back of his neck."

An account by Llewelyn Wyn Griffith, another eyewitness to this impromptu truce, says that after a night of exchanging carols, dawn on Christmas Day saw a "rush of men from both sides and a feverish exchange of souvenirs" before the men were called back by their officers. There were offers of a ceasefire for the day and a football match, but the brigade commander insisted they resume firing in the afternoon.

The high command was aghast when they heard about what was going on in the field. Both sides quickly issued strict orders against friendly communication with the enemy. All fraternization was forbidden. Interestingly, unlike most of the fighting men, a young corporal in the 16th Bavarian Reserve Infantry strongly opposed the truce. His name was Adolf Hitler.

## Later Unsanctioned Truces

Tentative feelers were put out in the following years by the Germans proposing a Christmas truce, but the British rebuffed them. Still unofficial truces did occur at scattered locations. Evidence of a Christmas truce in 1916 was found in a letter home by a 23-year-old Private, Ronald MacKinnon. He writes of German and Canadian soldiers reaching across the battle lines near Vimy Ridge to share Christmas greetings and trade presents. "Here we are again as the song says. I had quite a good Xmas considering I was in the front line. Xmas eve was pretty stiff, sentry-go up to the hips in mud of course...We had a truce on Xmas Day and our German friends were quite friendly. They came over to see us and we traded bully beef for cigars."

MacKinnon died shortly thereafter in the Battle of Vimy Ridge.

## Chapter Fifteen
## The Two Men Who Shaped Christmas

### Saint Francis of Assisi

The way in which the world celebrates Christmas can be traced back to the influence of two men...both of whom you know well. The first of the pair is the universal saint whose statue is so often seen in gardens because of his close association with animals. Yes, some of the most important religious traditions surrounding the Christmas season originated with St. Francis of Assisi. The traditions that Francis began have become so much a part of our celebrations of Christmas that it is now hard to imagine them ever not being there.

### How Things Were Before Francis

Although Christmas was part of the liturgical calendar with an established day of remembrance it had no elaborate rituals associated with it, especially in the Early Church. It was the 4th Century before it appeared in the list of Feasts and Festivals with its own defined liturgy. In 425 a Codex banned circus games on December 25th, but it was only in 529 that the cessation of work was imposed. The Second Council of Tours in 566-7, proclaimed the sanctity of the *twelve days* from Christmas to Epiphany and the duty of an Advent fast. Fasting was forbidden on Christmas Day and all of the faithful were required to receive communion. And so it remained for centuries. People typically celebrated Christmas by going to Mass at church, where they would here a sermon on the birth of the Christ Child. Churches occasionally had paintings of Jesus as an infant, but that was pretty much the extent of things.

## St. Francis has an New Idea

Everything changed when, in 1223, St. Francis invented the nativity scene. From that comes all of the little crèches we have in our homes, the larger sets they have in most churches, the outdoor displays with live animals. It all began with St. Francis.

St. Bonaventure, who entered the Franciscan Order of Friars Minor around 1240, wrote a biography of St. Francis of Assisi. Here's how he tells the story of the first Nativity Set: "It happened in the third year before his death, that in order to excite the inhabitants of Grecio to commemorate the nativity of the Infant Jesus with great devotion, Francis determined to keep it with all possible solemnity; and lest he should be accused of lightness or novelty, he asked and obtained the permission of the Pontiff.

Then he prepared a manger, and brought hay, and an ox and an ass to the place appointed. When the brethren were summoned, the people ran to join him. The forest resounded with their voices, and that venerable night was made glorious by many and brilliant lights and sonorous psalms of praise. The man of God stood before the manger, full of devotion and piety, bathed in tears and radiant with joy; the Holy Gospel was chanted by Francis, the Levite of Christ. Then he preached to the people around the nativity of the poor King; and being unable to utter His name for the tenderness of His love, he called Him the Babe of Bethlehem.

A certain valiant and veracious soldier, Master John of Grecio, who, for the love of Christ, had left the warfare of this world, and become a dear friend of this holy man, affirmed that he beheld an Infant marvelously beautiful, sleeping in the manger, Whom the blessed Father Francis embraced with both his arms, as if he would awake Him from sleep. This vision of the devout soldier is credible, not only by reason of the sanctity of him that saw it, but by reason of the miracles which afterwards confirmed its truth. For example of Francis, if it be considered by the world, is doubtless sufficient to excite all hearts which are negligent in the faith of Christ; and the hay of that manger, being preserved by the people, miraculously cured all diseases of cattle, and many other pestilences; God thus in all things glorifying his servant, and witnessing to the great efficacy of his holy prayers by manifest prodigies and miracles."

## The Increasing Popularity of Francis' Nativity Scene

Francis correctly understood that a realistic nativity scene would help people of that era, and forever after, imagine what it may have been like to be present on the first Christmas. He set it up in a cave just outside Greccio and featured costumed people playing the roles of Mary and Joseph. Local shepherds watched over their sheep in nearby fields, just as shepherds in Bethlehem watched over sheep on the first Christmas, when the sky suddenly filled with angels announcing Christ's birth.

This first nativity scene turned out to be so popular that people in other areas began setting up their own living nativities to celebrate Christmas. Eventually, Christians worldwide celebrated Christmas by visiting living nativity scenes and praying at nativity scenes made of statues in their town squares and churches.

It wasn't long before the nativity scene migrated from the outdoors into people's homes. Eventually small statues were created representing not only the Holy Family and the ox and ass, but also angels, shepherds, sheep, camels, and the three Wise Men that we have today.

## The Introduction of Christmas Carols

In addition to introducing the nativity scene, St. Francis also instituted the Christmas tradition of caroling. Prior to that time, people had listened to priests sing solemn Christmas hymns during formal church services. Francis, however, wanted people to be able to express their joy at Christmas by singing simple songs wherever they happened to be...at church, at home, or walking the fields doing their chores.

He based his idea on the Gospel of Luke. "Suddenly a great company of the heavenly host appeared with the angel, praising God and saying, 'And suddenly there was with the angel a multitude of the heavenly host praising God and saying, 'Glory to God in the highest, and on earth peace among men with whom he is pleased!'" (Luke 2:13-14). \ Francis felt that people should sing joyful songs of praise to God at Christmas just as the angels sang and praised God on the first Christmas.

One of St. Francis' special talents was finding simple, uncomplicated ways to transmit the message of Christ and salvation in a way the common folk could relate to. He did this by adding religious lyrics to the popular melodies of his time. In the process, he invented a new musical genre; he created what we now know as the Christmas carol. The word *carol*, by the way, is derived from the French word *caroler*, meaning dancing around in a circle.

Francis wrote a song called *"Psalmus in Nativitate"* for people to sing at Christmas. It was written in Latin so it could be sung during Mass, but had a popular melody. It was the first ever Christmas carol and led to the tradition of caroling that we all know and love today.

Wandering minstrels sang Christmas carols during the Middle Ages as they traveled from community to community. Mimicking this behavior, people formed groups and walked from door to door, singing Christmas carols for people at their doors. It wasn't long before people began rewarding these carolers with something warm to drink accompanied by snacks such as cookies.

Next time the radio stations begin playing Christmas music much too early, instead of fuming at them offer a quite prayer of thanks for St. Francis and the traditions he created.

**Charles Dickens**

In 1988, the Sunday Telegraph of London dubbed Charles Dickens *The Man Who Invented Christmas*. If you're not familiar with the history of Christmas celebrations, this may seem like an exaggeration. But on a closer examination, the Telegraph's phrase is closer to the truth than you might imagine.

In England at the turn of the nineteenth century, Christmas had almost vanished from the scene. The beginning of Victorian era in Britain marked a low ebb in the long decline of Christmas festivities. The energizing force that St Francis of Assisi brought to Christmas lasted until the 16th Century when things began to wane. It began with the Protestant Reformation in 1520, which stripped churches of decoration and shunned any practice deemed *Romish*. Then in the mid-1600's Oliver Cromwell, a self-styled Puritan Moses, came to power. The revolt he led suspected all religious celebration and suppressed such frivolity such as the singing of Carols. For a time all celebration of Christmas was outlawed in England.

However, the ultimate disappearance of Christmas from the English scene can be traced to the Industrial Revolution rather than Cromwell's Revolution. As large numbers of people left their ancestral villages and moved to the large cities, they left behind cultural traditions such as the celebration of Christmas. The bosses of these new factories weren't inclined to encourage a holiday that meant a day off from work, especially a day of *paid* vacation. Ebenezer Scrooge's reluctance to give Bob Cratchit a holiday on Christmas was typical of the times.

Despite of these obstacles and setbacks, there was a sudden, spontaneous revival of Christmas celebrations in Victorian times. A number of things seemed to happen at once. Victoria married a Saxon, and Prince Albert brought with him the German custom of decorating a Christmas tree. The singing of Christmas carols, which had all but disappeared at the turn of the century, suddenly became quite popular again. And the first Christmas cards also appeared in the 1840's. But more than anything, it was the Christmas stories of Charles Dickens, particularly his 1843 masterpiece, *A Christmas Carol*, that rekindled the joy of Christmas in both Britain and America.

This new and romantic notion of Christmas resulted in a number of changes. Christmas, which had been ignored, now turned into a major holiday. The celebration of Christmas became a one or two-day affair rather than the traditional twelve days of Christmas. It was also an occasion for family and close friends to gather for food, singing, and merriment. Before *A Christmas Carol*, turkey was uncommon on Christmas tables. After the book, it became the choice for Christmas dinner.

Dickens himself described the holidays as "a good time, a kind, forgiving, charitable, pleasant time; the only time I know of in the long calendar of the year, when men and women seem by one consent to open their shut-up hearts freely, and to think of other people below them as if they really were fellow-passengers to the grave..." For the rest of his life Dickens called it his *Carol Philosophy*.

He did not so much invent these traditions as resurrect and popularize them. Much of what we consider a traditional Christmas comes from the vision Dickens portrayed in *A Christmas Carol*. His name had become so synonymous with Christmas that on hearing of his death in 1870 a young girl in London asked her father, "With Mr. Dickens dead, does that mean Father Christmas will die as well?"

## Chapter Sixteen
## THE TWELVE DAYS OF CHRISTMAS

Christmas Day, known as the *Day of Nativity* in the Eastern Church, begins with the vigil Christmas Eve Mass. However, Christmas is more than just a day; it's also a season, traditionally known as Christmastide. Unlike the mercantile Christmas season, which now begins sometime between Halloween and Thanksgiving, and positively concludes at midnight December 24th so as not to intrude on the after-Christmas sales which begin the next day, Christmastide has always lasted from December 25th until the Baptism of our Lord, which is celebrated the Sunday following the Epiphany.

Nestled within Christmastide are two traditional festive seasons: the Octave of Christmas and the Twelve Days of Christmas. The Octave of Christmas (from the Latin *octava*, meaning eight) finds its roots in the Old Testament where many of the Hebrew's feasts and festivals lasted for eight days. The *Festival of Tabernacles*, Sukkoth, and the *Festival of Light*,

Chanukah, are two examples. Today the Church honors two festive seasons with an Octave, Easter and Christmas.

The Twelve Days of Christmas are counted from Christmas Day until the eve of the Epiphany, January 5th. Several notable feast days occur during this period. One of these is the Feast of St. Stephen which occurs the day after Christmas. Known as *Boxing Day* throughout the British Empire, it draws its name from the alms box in which worshippers deposited a gift for the poor on Christmas day. St. Stephen, you will recall, was one of the first deacons and his task was to make the daily distribution of food to the believers. The morning after Christmas, December 26th, the box was opened and the gifts distributed. We learn that this custom was not restricted to the British Isles from the Carol depicting a 10th Century Bohemian King distributing alms to the poor: *"Good King Wenceslas looked out on the feast of Stephen..."*

The Twelve Days of Christmas ends on the eve of the Epiphany or, as it is appropriately called, the Twelfth Night. During the Middle Ages the Twelve Days of Christmas became a time of revelry and foolishness. The Shakespearean play *Twelfth Night* is built around this celebration of Christmas madness and features one of his many wise fools who understand the real meaning of life better than those who think they are bright. In the United States, the celebration of the Epiphany has moved to the Sunday between January 2nd and January 8th, which lessened the festive significance of the 12 days by making the period variable.

And finally, while most everyone is familiar with the song *The Twelve Days of Christmas*, very few people are aware that it is, in fact, an allegorical rhyme designed as a memory aid. The date of the song's first performance has been lost to history, but it is found in European and Scandinavia traditions as early as the 16th century. Each of the items in the song is representational of a significant part of Christian teaching. The hidden meaning of each of the twelve gifts was designed to help youngsters learn their faith.

The repetitive nature of the song and the way it correlates

number of days and quantity of items makes it easy to remember and repeat even by the youngest child. he items themselves seem just eccentric enough, particularly to modern ears, to make them memorable as well.

Examining the song's allegorical underpinnings, we find that the *True Love* referred to in the song is God Himself. Meanwhile, the *me* who receives all of these wonderful presents is every baptized person. Mentally sing it again incorporating this new understanding of the words.

**Day 1** The partridge in a pear tree is Christ Jesus upon the Cross.

**Day 2** The two turtle doves represent the Old and New Testaments.

**Day 3** The three French hens stand for Faith, Hope and Love.

**Day 4** The four calling birds are the four evangelists, Matthew, Mark, Luke and John.

**Day 5** The five golden rings represent the first five books of the Bible, also called the Jewish *Torah*, Genesis, Exodus, Leviticus, Numbers and Deuteronomy.

**Day 6** The six geese a-laying are the six days of creation.

**Day 7** The seven swans a-swimming refers to the seven gifts of the Holy Spirit: Wisdom, Understanding, Counsel, Fortitude, Knowledge, Piety and Fear of the Lord.

**Day 8** The eight maids a-milking served to remind children of the eight beatitudes enumerated in the Sermon on the Mount.

**Day 9** The nine ladies dancing represented the nine fruits of the Holy Spirit found in Galatians: Love, Joy, Peace, Patience, Kindness, Goodness, Faithfulness, Gentleness and Self Control.

**Day 10** The ten lords a-leaping are the Ten Commandments.

**Day 11** The eleven pipers piping refers to the eleven faithful apostles.

**Day 12** The twelve drummers drumming were the twelve points of belief expressed in the Apostles' Creed: Belief in God the Father, the Son and the Holy Spirit, that Jesus Christ was born of the Virgin Mary, Made man, Crucified, Died and rose on the third day, that He sits at the right hand of the father and will come again, the Resurrection of the Dead and Life Everlasting.

One of the recurring themes of Christmas is its central place in most family traditions. Over time families have developed individual practices about particular foods, the time when the tree is decorated or when the presents are opened, how the Nativity set is arranged, and so on. None of these practices are good or bad. The important thing is the sense of cohesiveness and continuity they provide for children. It's surprising how often a discussion of Christmas around the water cooler devolves into a sharing of childhood memories.

An oft heard phrase these days is *Pay it Forward*. There's no better opportunity to do just that than filling your children's lives with many happy memories of Christmas. Don't be afraid to start a tradition or two of your own. Someday they'll thank you for it.

## Chapter Seventeen

## Favorite Christmas Songs

What is said to be the first Christmas hymn, *Veni redemptor gentium,* O come, Redeemer of the Earth, is attributed to St. Ambrose who was Archbishop of Milan in the 4th Century. Despite his efforts, as we saw in the previous chapter the singing of Christmas hymns, or Carols, by the common folk didn't become popular until the 13th Century. Since then, hundreds, perhaps thousands, of Carols both religious and secular have been written.

Yet even with this bounty of Carols to choose from, it seems that as each Christmas rolls around we hear pretty much the same tunes. Why? Probably because Christmas is built on traditions and nothing illicits childhood memories of Christmas like the old songs. Still, every so often a new one makes its way onto the list of favorites, *The Little Drummer Boy* being an example.

In an effort to play off the season, every year newspapers, radio and TV stations and websites poll their readers/listeners to produce their own top ten list of favorite Christmas Carols. After doing a little research, we now share the results of some of those surveys with you.

## The Top Ten Religious Carols

**1. *The Twelve Days of Christmas*** — This song may be one of the most surprising additions to this list since *The Twelve Days of Christmas,* as we have learned. was written in England as one of the catechism songs to help young Catholics learn the basics of their faith.

**2. *Silent Night*** — This very famous song, like *Oh Christmas Tree*, has its own origins from the German tradition where it is well known as *Stille Nacht*. This is the most translated song with over 147 versions.

**3. *Away in a Manger*** — The music to this song was written by James R. Murray but the lyrics remain an unknown. The words were found in a Lutheran Sunday school book published in 1885, in Philadelphia. While the song was thought to have German origins dating from the time of Martin Luther, it has since been proven that it does not.

**4. *The First Noel*** — This Christmas carol has English descent. An interesting fact is that its original spelling was *Nowell*. Some scholars believe the word to actually stand for the phrase, *Now all is well*. It was written sometime in the 17th Century and has been popular for over three centuries. Yet who first wrote the words or the music for this carol is unknown. It was passed down orally until finally written down in a book of Christmas carols in 1833.

**5. *God Rest Ye Merry Gentlemen*** — The traditional English hymn, *God Rest Ye Merry Gentlemen,* was termed "the most popular of Christmas carols" by the 19th Century newspaper editor, A.H. Bullen. The lyrics and music are simply credited as English Traditional with no known author.

**6. *It Came Upon a Midnight Clear*** — This song first started as a poem and Christmas carol written by Edmund Sears, pastor of the Unitarian Church in Weston, Massachusetts. Records show that it first appeared on December 29, 1849 in the Christian Register in Boston. In 1850 Richard Storrs Willis, a composer who trained under Felix Mendelssohn supplied the melody.

**7. *Joy to the World*** — Isaac Watts wrote this unforgettable carol back in 1719. Watts was an ordained Pastor of an Independent congregation. He also wrote many hymns and carols and was awarded a Doctor of Divinity degree by the University of Edinburgh in 1728. The music to the carol is by George Frederick Handel.

**8. *O Come all ye Faithful*** — The Englishman, John Francis Wade, wrote both the words and music, to the hymn known as *Adeste Fideles*. The musical score was not published until 1782. The lyrics were first published in 1760. It is definitely of English origin, despite its original Latin verses.

**9. *O come, O come, Emmanuel*** — This song is actually a translation of another Latin text, *Veni, veni, Emmanuel*, done by

John Mason Neale in the mid-19th Century. It is believed that the traditional sounding music stems from a 15th Century French processional for Franciscan nuns though other experts believe it may be 8th Century Gregorian in its origins. It is known as one of the most solemn Advent hymns.

**10.** *We Three Kings* — *We Three Kings of Orient Are* is a Christmas carol written by Reverend John Henry Hopkins, Jr., in 1857. He wrote both the words and the music as part of a Christmas pageant for the General Theological Seminary in New York City. It first appeared in his book *Carols, Hymns and Song* in 1863.

### A Secular List

ASCAP, the American Society of Composers, Authors and Publishers who license broadcast music developed a list of most-played songs over the holiday season. The list, of course, is limited to the songs they license. Based on over 2,500 radio stations nationwide, they compiled the following list.

**1.** *Sleigh Ride* by Leroy Anderson & Mitchell Parish.

**2.** *Winter Wonderland* by Felix Bernard & Richard B. Smith.

**3.** *The Christmas Song* (Chestnuts Roasting on an Open Fire) by Mel Tormé & Robert Wells.

**4.** *Let It Snow! Let It Snow! Let It Snow!* by Sammy Cahn & Jule Styne.

**5.** *Jingle Bell Rock* by Joseph Carleton Beal & James Ross Boothe.

**6.** *It's The Most Wonderful Time Of The Year* by Edward Pola & George Wyle.

**7.** *Do You Hear What I Hear?* by Gloria Shayne Baker.

**8.** *It's Beginning To Look A Lot Like Christmas* by Meredith Willson.

**9.** *Have Yourself A Merry Little Christmas* by Ralph Blane & Hugh Martin.

**10.** *Rudolph The Red Nosed Reindeer* by Johnny Marks.

## A Radio Station's Top Twenty

1. *The Christmas Song*
2. *Have Yourself a Merry Little Christmas*
3. *Winter Wonderland*
4. *Santa Claus Is Coming to Town*
5. *White Christmas*
6. *Let It Snow! Let It Snow! Let It Snow!*
7. *Jingle Bell Rock*
8. *The Little Drummer Boy*
9. *Sleigh Ride*
10. *Rudolph the Red-Nosed Reindeer*
11. *It's the Most Wonderful Time of the Year*
12. *I'll Be Home for Christmas*
13. *Silver Bells*
14. *Rockin' Around the Christmas Tree*
15. *Feliz Navidad*
16. *Blue Christmas*
17. *Frosty the Snowman*
18. *A Holly Jolly Christmas*
19. *It's Beginning To Look a Lot Like Christmas*
20. *I Saw Mommy Kissing Santa Claus*

What songs would be on *your* list? Our choice of favorite Christmas song is definitely driven by many factors...childhood memories ranking high among them. One newspaper took things a little further by asking participants to name the song they most *liked* along with the one they most *disliked*. Using this data, they compiled two separate lists. Interestingly enough, one song ended as number one on both lists. Its name? *The Christmas Song*, most often referred to by its opening line "Chestnuts roasting on an open fire..."

In closing, we present a short list of songs voted the most annoying. Feel free to add one that you think should be on the list. In no particular order, here they are:

***Jingle Bells by the Four Barking Dogs***
***I saw Mommy Kissing Santa***
***The Chipmunks Christmas Song***
***Grandma got run over by a Reindeer***
***Christmas Shoes***
***All I want for Christmas is My Two Front Teeth***
***I want a Hippopotamus for Christmas***

## *Chapter Eighteen*

## A MOST UNUSUAL CHRISTMAS CAROL

Mention a Christmas tale about a crotchety old man who disliked people until he had some other worldly visions on Christmas Eve and everyone immediately thinks of Charles Dickens' perennially popular story featuring Ebenezer Scrooge, Bob Cratchit, Tiny Tim and Marley's Ghost. As well they should. *A Christmas Carol* was published on December 19, 1843 and the entire print run sold out in just four days. The book became an instant hit, and in no time at all people all across England and the United States knew and loved the story. It's still beloved today.

### The Probable Origins of Ebenezer Scrooge

While everyone knows about Scrooge's miserly ways, the Ghost of Christmas Past and Christmas Future, etc., few people are familiar with the name Gabriel Grub. In 1836, a full seven years before Dickens wrote *A Christmas Carol*, he produced a short story as Chapter 29 of The Pickwick Papers. Called *The Story of the Goblins who Stole a Sexton*, it tells the eerie story of Gabriel Grub, the Sexton (caretaker and gravedigger) of a small rural church. Dickens describes him as "...an ill-conditioned, cross-grained, surly fellow – a morose and lonely man, who consorted with nobody but himself." Grub had "a deep scowl of malice and ill-humor." Sound like anyone you know?

### A Rather Morose Man this Gabriel Grub

One fateful Christmas Eve, Gabriel Grub sets out for the church yard with his pick and shovel to dig a grave. As he walks through the town, "he notes all the people making preparations for Christmas celebrations...celebrations he despised and would refuse to partake in should he ever be invited, which, of course, he never was. He passes children and happily thinks of, measles, scarlet fever, thrush, whooping-cough, and a good many other sources of consolations besides."

Anyone who offered him a Christmas greeting received a "a short, sullen growl" in return. This is clearly a precursor to Scrooge's more famous "Humbug!" When Grub comes across a young boy singing carols on the street corner he "rapped him over the head with his lantern five or six times." He composes his own little ditty as he walks to the graveyard, "A coffin at Christmas! A Christmas box! Ho! ho! ho!"

## Suddenly Life Changes

Gabriel Grub's miserable life turns upside down when he receives a strange visitor, a grinning goblin who taunts him and is quickly joined by "a whole troop of goblins." They take Grub captive and drag him down into the earth. He finds himself in a cavern with the "king of goblins," and his band. They show him a series of scenes magically projected on the end of the cavern. The first scene is a poor family. The children and their mother are waiting for the man of the house to return. They celebrate when, at long last, their father joins them. The scene shifts to a bedroom, where "the fairest and youngest child lay dying," Dickens tells us, "Even as the sexton looked upon him with an interest he had never felt or known before, the little boy died." Yet the family took solace, since their little one was in "happy Heaven."

It's impossible not to see the Cratchit family and Tiny Tim in this scene.

The goblins then proceed to give Grub a series of beatings, each interspersed with new scenes. In this way, "many a lesson is taught to Gabriel Grub. He saw that men who worked hard, and earned their scanty bread with lives of labor, were cheerful and happy because they bore within their own bosoms the materials of happiness, contentment, and peace." Meanwhile, Grub "saw that men like himself, who snarled at the mirth and cheerfulness of others, were the foulest weeds on the fair surface of the earth, and setting all the good of the world against the evil, he came to the conclusion that it was a very decent and respectable sort of world after all."

The beatings eventually conclude and Grub falls asleep. He awakens in the churchyard on Christmas morning. After his encounter with the goblins, he "was an altered man. Yet he could not bear the thought of returning to a place where his repentance would be scoffed at, and his reformation disbelieved."

Rather than face his neighbors, Gabriel Grub vanishes for ten years. He finally returns as "a ragged, contented, rheumatic old man." The moral of the story, according to the narrator, was "that if a man turn sulky and drinks by himself at Christmas time, he may make up his mind to be not a bit the better for it: let the spirits be never so good."

## Peering over the Author's Shoulder

One can't help but feel that they've been given an opportunity to look over Charles Dickens' shoulder and share in the development of his literary epic, *A Christmas Carol*. The similarities between *The Story of the Goblins* and *A Christmas Carol* are easily apparent: a solitary, nasty old man not only refuses to celebrate Christmas, but also spurns the greetings of those who do, and even tries to hurt a boy who sings a Christmas carol. On Christmas Eve, unexpected supernatural visitors show him many scenes of life that cut him to the quick. As a result, the experience changes his outlook forever after.

The greatest difference between the two tales is the protagonist's reaction to the supernatural events. On the one hand, we have Gabriel Grub who leaves town rather than face the ridicule of his neighbors. On the other, we have Ebenezer Scrooge who, faced with the dreadful sight of his own demise, decides, "I will honor Christmas in my heart, and try to keep it all the year. I will live in the Past, the Present, and the Future. The Spirits of all Three shall strive within me. I will not shut out the lessons that they teach."

Dickens writes: "Scrooge was better than his word. He did it all, and infinitely more; and to Tiny Tim, who did not die, he was a second father. He became as good a friend, as good a master, and as good a man, as the good old city knew, or any other good old city, town, or borough, in the good old world. Some people laughed to see the alteration in him, but he let them laugh, and little heeded them; for he was wise enough to know that nothing ever happened on this globe, for good, at which some people did not have their fill of laughter in the outset; and knowing that such as these would be blind anyway, he thought it quite as well that they should wrinkle up their eyes in grins, as have the malady in less attractive forms. His own heart laughed: and that was quite enough for him."

Why was one character (Scrooge) able to transcend the fear of his neighbors' reaction while the other (Grub) ran from it? What are we to make of the different way in which the two stories conclude? Could it indicate a fundamental change in Dickens' thinking? Had he perhaps turned the story over in his mind and decided he could do better by his character?

That seems to have been the case. Of course he wrote *A Christmas Carol* because he needed the income, but it also gave him a second opportunity to perfect and complete his message that we often require an agent beyond ourselves (grace, if you will) to become the person we were meant to be.

## *Chapter Nineteen*
## WAS THERE A GOOD KING WENCESLAUS?

**Statue of Wenceslaus in Prague**

At one time or another most of us have sung, or at the very least heard, the Christmas Carol *Good King Wenceslaus*—

Good King Wenceslaus looked out, on the Feast of Stephen,

When the snow lay round about, deep and crisp and even.

It's hard to even read those lyrics without having the forceful thump of the melody echo in your brain. Be that as it may, the question remains...Was there *really* a King named Wenceslaus? And more importantly, was he good? The answer is yes on both counts. With those issues out of the way, it seems appropriate to delve deeper.

Let's deal with the second question first. Goodness. He is counted among the saints by both the Western and Eastern Church. Saint Wenceslaus is the patron saint of Bohemia.

Although a ruler, Wenceslaus I was, in fact, not a King but a Duke. He was made a Duke by the Emperor Otto I, and ruled Bohemia, a historic region in central Europe, which occupies the western two-thirds of the modern Czech Republic. The country's capitol was Prague.

## Who Were The Bohemians?

Like so much of Europe, the name *Bohemia* originated with the Romans. In the 2nd century BC, the Romans were competing for dominance of northern Italy with various peoples, including a tribe known as the Boii. The Romans defeated the Boii at the Battle of Placentia in 194 BC and again at the Battle of Mutina in 193 BC. After this, many of the Boii retreated north across the Alps.

Later Roman authors refer to the area they went to as *Boihaemum*. The earliest mention occurs in Tacitus' *Germania 28,* which was written nearly three centuries later. The name given to the people combines the tribal name *Boii* with the Germanic element *xaim*. *Xiam* later became *haims*, in German *heim*, and in English *home*. (In other words, the home of the Boii.)This original *Boihaemum* as Tacitus called it, included parts of southern Bohemia as well as parts of Bavaria and Austria. The name *Czech* or *Čechy* is derived from the name of the Slavic tribe of Czechs that settled the area in 6th or 7th century.

Initially, Bohemia was a part of Greater Moravia. The latter, weakened by years of internal conflict and constant warfare, ultimately succumbed and fragmented due to the continual invasions by the nomadic Magyars. However, Bohemia remained part of the Moravian Empire long enough for a large portion of the population to become Christians.

Wenceslaus was the son of Vratislaus I, Duke of Bohemia during the Přemyslid dynasty. His father was raised in a Christian environment and purportedly Saints Cyril and Methodius converted Wenceslaus' grandfather, Borivoj I of Bohemia.

## Wenceslaus Comes to Power

The missionaries, Saints Cyril and Methodius, managed to

convert the Czech Prince Borivoy and his wife Ludmilla, but the faith was not necessarily transmitted to their subjects. Many powerful Czechs were against the introduction of Christianity in Bohemia since it threatened the privileges and powers of their own pagan religion.

Borivoy and Ludmilla's son, Prince Vratislav, married a woman named Dragomir, the daughter of a pagan tribal chieftain. Their first son, whom we know as Wenceslaus, was born near Prague around 907. The couple had four daughters as well as another son, Boleslaus. In 921, when Wenceslaus was thirteen, his father was killed in battle and Otto I confirmed him as his father's successor. Fearing the negative influence of his pagan mother, his grandmother Ludmila, stepped in as regent and raised Wenceslaus as a Christian.

Meanwhile, the same nobles who'd objected to Christianity began to encourage Dragomir to reclaim her son saying, "Your son is better fit for a monastery than a throne." They eventually developed a plan to eliminate his Grandmother's influence and had Ludmilla strangled. The evil mother reclaimed her son and forced him to participate in pagan rituals.

Wenceslaus, however, secretly continued celebrating his Christian faith in private services late at night. Dragomir's actions turned the people against her. The eventually fomented an uprising, deposing and banishing her. Wenceslaus turned eighteen about this time and took the throne. Ever the good Christian, he heeded the commandment to honor one's father and mother and recalled Dragomir to the castle.

The young man developed a reputation as a good and fair ruler who, to protect his people, on one occasion volunteered to face some marauders in hand-to-hand combat and let the outcome settle their dispute. He was said to be generous to all, giving clothing those in need, providing shelter to wayfarers and pilgrims, and using his own funds to ransom those sold into slavery. He constructed Christian churches throughout the duchy. The pagan nobles not only rejected his religious beliefs, but objected to his friendship with Christian King Henry I, "the

Fowler," of Germany. Wenceslas believed Henry to be the rightful heir of Charlemagne and sought his friendship to avoid having the Germans take his country by force.

## Wenceslaus Dies

Troubles continued to escalate between the Christian Prince and his pagan nobility. Things reached a head on September 28, 935 when, at Dragomir's urging, he was assassinated by his younger brother, Boleslaus the Cruel. After murdering Wenceslaus, he hacked his brother's body to pieces and buried it at Alt-Bunzlau.

Tradition says Wenceslaus' murder occurred during a feast held at the same time as Boleslaus' son was born. Possible verification for this legend might be found in the fact that the son received the strange name of Strachkvaus, which means *dreadful feast*.

Boleslaus repented three years later and had Wencelaus' body moved to the Church of St. Vitus in Prague. Apparently remorseful for what he had done, he also vowed to educate his son as a clergyman. The murderous brother ruled Bohemia for 32 years until his death on July 15, 967. He is generally respected by Czech historians as an energetic ruler who strengthened the Bohemian state and expanded its territory. Ambition, rather than the pro-Christian religious policies pursued by his elder brother, may have been the motivation for Boleslaus' fratricide. During his rule he never impeded the growth of Christianity in Bohemia, and actually sent his daughter, a nun, to the Pope to ask permission to make Prague a bishopric.

After his death, Wenceslaus was viewed as a martyr and his concern for the poor led to him being revered as a holy person. His reputation for heroic goodness resulted in his elevation to sainthood. Saint Wenceslaus was posthumously declared king and named patron saint of the Czech state. A catchy tune extolling Good King Wenceslaus' pious deeds was sung by the Czech people every spring as a springtime song celebrating nature's powers of rebirth. Almost a thousand years after Wenceslaus's murder, a 19th-century Englishman named John

Mason Neale wrote the now-famous English lyrics for the ancient melody.

## St. Wenceslaus' Final Resting Place

St. Wenceslaus' body remains where Boleslaus put it; in the St. Wenceslaus Chapel at the Cathedral of St. Vitus. The decorations in the chapel are priceless. The lower parts of the walls are covered with gold and decorated with more than 1,300 gems. The walls contain 2,500 square feet of frescoes depicting scenes from Wenceslaus's life. St. Wenceslaus' tomb stands at the center of the chapel.

This next part sounds like something out of a Dan Brown novel. There is a special door in the southwest corner of the chapel. Behind the door is a staircase leading to the Coronation chamber where the Crown Jewels of the Czech Republic are stored. Among other things, they include the St. Wenceslaus Crown of Charles IV, dated from 1347; a Royal Scepter and Orb both from the first half of the 16th century, and the Coronation Vestments including the grand Coronation Cloak dating from the early 17th century.

Behind the door to the Coronation chamber is the door of an iron safe. Between them, these two doors have seven locks, which require seven separate keys. These seven keys are kept by seven different people, who must all be brought together for the door to be opened. The holders of the keys are Czechoslovakia's President, the Prime Minister, the Archbishop of Prague, the Chairman of the House of Deputies, the Chairman of the Senate, the Dean of St. Vitus Cathedral, and the Lord Mayor of Prague. The Coronation chamber was opened only nine times in the 20th century. Presumably, like Wenceslaus, everything is still there.

## *Chapter Twenty*
## THE WISE MEN COME CALLING

### The Magi as Depicted in Art

Before we address those stalwarts of every Nativity Set, the Wise Men, also known as the Magi, there are a few misconceptions that need to be laid to rest. Nearly everyone is familiar with the standard division of the Gospels into the three (Matthew, Mark and Luke) Synoptic Gospels [from the Greek *syn* — together and *opsis* — appearance] and the Gospel of John.

Instead, consider dividing the Gospels into those that provide a birth narrative and those that do not. This splits them down the middle with Matthew and Luke on the *do have* side and Mark and John on the *don't have* side. Both Matthew (20%) and Luke (35%) offer a considerable amount of unique information and nowhere is it more apparent than in their birth narratives. Matthew ignores the shepherds in favor of the Wise Men, whereas Luke does just the opposite.

Over time, the Magi have been imagined to have been everything from traveling entertainers, to magicians, to kings. Yes Kings. All together now, "We Three Kings from Orient are..." However, all Matthew says is, "...in the days of Herod the King, behold, wise men (in Greek ἀγός, that is, Magos...an Oriental scientist or *Wise Man*) from the east came to Jerusalem..."

A standard Nativity Set comes with three Wise Men although Matthew never mentioned any numbers in his Gospel. In Medieval times there were sometimes thought to be as many as a dozen Wise Men. What Matthew does say is that they brought *three* gifts and this is what led to conclusion that there must have been three of them.

History has given them various names. Hormizdah, Yazdegerd and Perozdh are mentioned in one account. In another, they are called, Hor, Basanater and Karsudan. The Western tradition names them Balthazar, Melchior and Gaspar. In a 6th Century mosaic, Balthazar is middle aged and has a black beard, Gaspar is old with a white beard and Melchior is young and beardless.

**Map of Roman Empire and Parthia**

Notice also that Matthew says they all came from the same place, the east. Yet a typical Nativity always includes one black Wise Man. This is because a tradition developed that they represented all three races...i.e. the entirety of mankind. Balthasar was often portrayed as an Asian, Gaspar a white European and Melchior an African and therefore black. Their ages and races have tended to vary. In reality Africa is south and west of Israel, so if they came from the east they couldn't have been African.

Interestingly enough, Magoi – the original phrase Matthew used – was the title given to members of the upper house of the Parthian Government and advisors to Phraates, ruler of the Parthian Dynasty. And that camel stuff? They may have used camels for baggage, but Parthians were more than likely to have traveled on horseback. The Parthians were known as expert horsemen and their cavalry routinely outflanked and defeated the Roman army. Combine that with the fact that the Province of Syria formed the Eastern edge of the Roman Empire and bordered the Parthian Empire.

Parthia's influence extended from there to the Indus River. The Parthians also had a history of meddling in Jewish politics. Prior to Herod the Great gaining the Jewish throne they supported Herod's rival, Hyrcanus II, a Hasmonean claimant. A civil war of sorts was fought over the right to rule the Jews. Herod's brother, Phesaelus, was killed in this fighting and Herod and his family were very nearly captured. As a matter of fact, Josephus writes that at one point Herod was so demoralized that he was ready to commit suicide.

Parthia's capitol was Babylon, home to a large contingent of Jews who were very familiar with Daniel's prophecies of a coming Mashiach. And, finally, Matthew says the Magi followed a star to Bethlehem. The Parthians themselves were Zorastrians and strong believers in astrologic influences.

From this evidence one could reasonably conclude that the Magi, or Wise Men, were Magoi from Parthia sent on a diplomatic mission to investigate the possible fulfillment of prophecies relating to the coming birth of the Jewish Mashiach.

One final point. Even though statues of the Wise Men are included in every Nativity set and nearly everyone puts them in the stable along with the shepherds, most experts agree they arrived much later. Since Jesus was a firstborn son, Mary and Joseph would have had to make trips to the Temple to ransom him back and then again for Mary's purification. She had family ties in Judea and Joseph may have had as well, so it only makes sense that they would have chosen to remain in Bethlehem to complete these requirements. Matthew also refers to the Wise Men visiting the Christ Child in a house and, when the Holy Family had to flee to Egypt, they clearly left from Judea not Nazareth. All of this leads to the conclusion that Jesus was most probably a toddler by the time the Wise Men arrived.

This separation of time and place is also seen in the celebration of the feast of the Epiphany. This is the Christian feast day that celebrates the revelation of God the Son as a human being in Jesus Christ. Closing out the Christmas season, it falls on January 6th, but is typically celebrated on the Sunday between January 2nd and January 8th. The Western Church traditionally commemorates the visitation of the Magi, i.e., his manifestation to the Gentiles, on this day.

## Chapter Twenty-One
## Epiphany — The Gentile Christmas

Two important Feast Days occur during the 12-day Christmas season and, because Christmas is a fixed date in the liturgical calendar, all other Feasts in the Christmas season are also fixed. The first of these is the Feast of the Circumcision on January 1st.

The Torah states, "This is my covenant, which you shall keep, between me and you and your descendants after you. Every male among you shall be circumcised." (Gen 17:10) Likewise, Leviticus 12:3 says, "And on the eighth day the flesh of his foreskin shall be circumcised."

For a child born on the 25th of December, the eighth day would be January, 1st. The day of circumcision was also the day on which the child was named. Recall the somewhat comical scene surrounding the naming of John the Baptist in Luke 1:59-64. "And on the eighth day they came to circumcise the child; and they would have named him Zechariah after his father, but his mother said, "Not so; he shall be called John." And they said to her, "None of your kindred is called by this name." And they made signs to his father, inquiring what he would have him called. And he asked for a writing tablet, and wrote, "His name is John." And they all marveled. And immediately his mouth was opened and his tongue loosed, and he spoke, blessing God."

The second of these Feast Days is the Feast of the Epiphany...from the Greek ἐπιφάνεια, *epiphaneia* — appearance or manifestation. An epiphany is a sudden realization about the nature or meaning of something. This Feast celebrates the revelation of the Christ along with the appearance of the Magi. The prophet, Isaiah, anticipated their coming when he wrote, "A multitude of camels shall cover you, the young camels of Midian and Ephah; all those from Sheba shall come. They shall bring gold and frankincense and shall proclaim the praise of the LORD."(Is 6:60) Likewise, Balaam, the prophet hired by the King of Moab to curse Israel said, "...a star shall come forth out of Jacob, and a scepter shall rise out of Israel..." (Num 24:17)

The Epiphany is a season of light and joy, a time of offering praise to God who did not leave mankind in darkness but sent his Son with the good news of salvation. The gifts we give at Christmas are done in imitation of the Magi. However, there is one important difference; the Magi brought gifts to Jesus, not each other. So even as the Christmas lights are coming down, the light of Christ continues to shine down on us and we are called to reflect that light. "Let your light so shine before men that they may see your good works and give glory to your Father in heaven."(Matt 5:16)

We spoke earlier of an epiphany being an infusion of knowledge, a sudden realization. Through the Epiphany we are led to understand that Jesus Christ came not merely as King of the Jews, but King of the world and all that is in it. Just as those few shepherds were representative of the Jewish nation, in coming to Bethlehem the Magi represent the rest of mankind. If one views Christmas as the manifestation of the birth of the Messiah to the Jews, then the Epiphany can be seen as its Gentile equivalent...a Gentile Christmas, if you will. The underlying message of the Epiphany, of the Magi, is that Jesus Christ came not to save a select few, but all of mankind.

## Chapter Twenty-Two

## HERE COME THE MUMMERS

**Ghouls and a Jester-like Devil in the Mummer Parade**

On New Year's Day everyone on the West Coast lines up in sunny Pasadena to watch the Rose Parade. Meanwhile, on the other side of the continent folks in Philadelphia, despite the frigid weather, are enjoying their own event, the Mummers' Parade.

The Mummers and their parade continue a tradition that extends back to about 400 BC and the Roman Festival of Saturnalia. A time of topsy-turvy turn around, during Saturnalia the slaves became the masters and the masters the slaves. People wore masks, celebrated with charades and satire, sang and danced in the streets, and exchanged gifts. When the Roman Empire forced its way into Britannia, the Celts and Druids gave the festival their own twist. Time passed, and by the Middle Ages this day of festivity had become an integral part of most Christmas celebrations.

The word Mummer comes from the term for silence...as in Mum's the word. Going further back in history, we find the ancient Greek god, Momus, who was the personification of mockery, blame, ridicule, scorn, and stinging criticism. In Greek mythology Momus was expelled from heaven for criticizing and ridiculing the other gods. In other words, Momus was silenced.

Before the festival moved to New Year's Day, boys trapped a wren on St. Stephen's Day (December 26th) and killed it. A legend held that St. Stephen hid from his attackers in a bush and his position was given away by a wren perched in the branches. The boys were punishing the wren for its part in the stoning of St. Stephen 1,500 or so years earlier. Having killed the wren, the boys tied its body to a stick and blackened their faces with charcoal, presumably so they wouldn't be recognized. Then they went door to door in a sort of trick or treat mode, waving the dead bird in people's faces and waiting for them to give them some reward. You'll be happy to know that in the few places where this part of the festival is still reenacted, they now use a fake bird.

A second part of the celebration is the presence of Morris Dancers or Mummers. These groups dressed in wildly outrageous costumes and performed what came to be called the Mummer's Play. The play's cast consists of a King, usually Saint George, who expresses the need to kill someone, typically a Saracen knight. Saracen was a term used by the ancient Romans to refer to a people, ethnically distinct from the Arabs, who inhabited the deserts near the Roman province of Syria. One of earliest references to them is in Ptolemy's Geography, in which he uses the Greek term *Sarakenoi* when referring to a non-Arabic people living in the northwestern Arabian peninsula.

In Christian writing, the name came to be interpreted to mean "*those empty of Sarah*" or "*not from Sarah.*" In the Eighth Century St. John of Damascus wrote, "There is also a people-deceiving cult of the Ishmaelites, the forerunner of the Antichrist, which prevails until now. It derives from Ishmael, who was born to Abraham from Hagar, wherefore they are called Hagarenes and Ishmaelites. And we call them Saracens, inasmuch as they were sent away empty-handed by Sarah; for it was said to the angel by Hagar, 'Sarah has sent me away empty-handed.'"

Returning to our play; as it turns out, just such a Saracen Knight happens to be available, often with the name of Slasher. The two go at it until Slasher is mortally wounded. At this point, either Slasher's mother appears, wailing for a doctor, or the King George character has a change of heart and requests the aid of a doctor himself. The call goes out for a ten dollar doctor, but a voice from offstage replies, "There is no ten dollar doctor." The request is then changed to a five dollar doctor. The less expensive doctor appears and cures the injured Knight.

While the play itself is still "performed" in some parts of England, Mummers in Philadelphia have opted for a lavish, and suitably garish, parade instead. Their huge fan of feathers and electric colors brings to mind Rio de Janeiro's *Carnaval* rather than a Medieval morality play, though the Mummers Parade features decidedly fewer women and no nudity. They have also dispensed with the now politically incorrect blackface.

The Mummers has a long and proud history in the city of Brotherly Love. Reports of rowdy groups *parading* on New Year's Day in Philadelphia date back to before the American Revolution. Prizes were offered by merchants in the late 1800's. In January, 1901 the first official parade offered about $1,725 in prize money from the city.

The Mummers Parade is serious business in Philadelphia. Like its Western counterpat, The Rose Parade, clubs and organizations work on the costumes and practice all year for their one day in the sun, or as is the case in Philadelphia, the wind, rain and/or snow. Performances and costumes are judged and there is a complicated set of rules the marchers must follow during the judging.

## About the Author:

Writing has always been a major part of E. G Lewis' life. A former newspaper editor and publisher, his articles have appeared in many national and regional magazines. He also wrote and directed corporate training films. Mr. Lewis writes both Commercial and Biblical Fiction as well as Non-Fiction. He began work on the Seeds of Christianity™ Series in 2008. The first book, **WITNESS**, was published in December, 2009. The second in the series, **DISCIPLE**, came out in June, 2010. The third book, **APOSTLE**, was released in April, 2011 and book four, **MARTYR,** appeared in February, 2012. He also has a number of Christian and general interest Non-Fiction Books. The first volumes in his Rome eBook series are slated for 2013. He also has published two Contemporary Suspense novels, *PROMISES* and *LOST.*

Mr. Lewis has a graduate degree in Economics from Ohio State University and worked in management and corporate planning before becoming a fulltime novelist. He and his wife Gail, also a writer and editor, live on the Southern Oregon Coast.

## Chapter Twenty-Three
## The Christmas Story from *WITNESS*
## Book One of The Seeds of Christianity™ Series

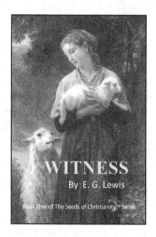

### Synopsis

As a young shepherdess, Rivkah, accompanies her father to Bethlehem where, with Mary's help, she holds baby Jesus. But Mary, Joseph and Jesus are soon gone and Herod's soldiers begin killing the children of Rivkah's village. Then her intended, Shemu'el, is dragged away into slavery. Divided by fate, united by love, these two young people grow to separate adulthood, each with their dreams and desires unfulfilled, while the world of Rome and conquest moves inexorably on.

Rivkah eventually marries and raises a family. Life is good until the day she encounters Jesus a final time...this time on his way to crucifixion. She follows and this time, as they take him from the cross, it's Rivkah who helps Mary hold her son. A first century epic tale of love lost and love found, the series is Biblically and historically accurate.

Rivkah goes to the stable in Bethlehem, a 21-page Bonus Excerpt taken from *WITNESS,* the first book in E. G. Lewis' best-selling Seeds of Christianity Series™, begins on the following page.

## ~ 6 ~

*"And in that region there were shepherds out in the field, keeping watch over their flock at night."* —Luke 2:8

I named my sheep *Liat*, which means *You are mine*. Having a sheep all my own made going to the fields much more exciting. I still did womanly chores with Aunt Tamar, but as soon as Abba returned with the flock, my feet flew out the door as I ran to check on Liat. Now I had two things to think about while sweeping, grinding meal and kneading dough, Liat and Shemu'el. Well, mostly Shemu'el.

But for a time there would be no more weaving and dyeing, sweeping and stitching for Rivkah. Lambing season had come and, as a shepherdess, my duty was to be with my flock. Abba and I would spend our nights in the field along with Shemu'el, his brothers and father and the other shepherds of our settlement. I danced with excitement as I scurried around the house preparing to leave.

Abba moved the sheep to the birthing pasture about the ninth hour, leaving me behind to gather the things we needed. My bag waited, stuffed with food. Knowing the fields grew cold at night, I threw in our fleece-lined cloaks. After tucking my rod into my sash, I glanced around the room making a final check. Ready to go. I tossed the bag over my shoulder, grabbed my staff and bid my cousins in the next house farewell.

My heart pounded with anticipation as I skipped down the path. The coolness of the coming evening settled around me on my way to the pasture. A surprisingly large number of people traveled the main road heading for Bethlehem. I threaded my way between them watching the setting sun paint pink and purple bands across the western sky.

I had slipped my *shrika* into my leather purse in hopes of playing it when we sang around the fire. A quick pat verified it was still there. My feet could not get me there fast enough.

By the time I reached the fields, the sky had turned dusky blue-gray and a delicate rim of moon peaked over the mountains behind me. Wispy ribbons of smoke rose from the valley; they had already lit the evening's fire. Abba noticed me walking along the crest of the hill and dashed up to meet me.

"Good news," he said, breathless from the climb.

Seeing his wide grin filled me with happiness.

"Lambing season has begun, my little dove. Just before you arrived the first ewe dropped a pair of healthy rams."

"Perhaps those twins are the omen of a prosperous season."

"May the Lord make it so."

I took his hand as we walked. "Why are there so many pilgrims on the road? It is not a time for festivals, and Pesach is not until the month of Nisan."

"Those are not pilgrims, they are going to Bethlehem for the census." Seeing my confusion, he explained. "Some time ago Caesar Augustus ordered a count of the whole world. They do it by province, beginning in the west and moving to the east."

He shrugged. "Our turn has come. It is about taxation and gathering gold. Just another Roman scheme to squeeze the last drops out of a rag they have already wrung dry."

"Do they not have enough already?"

Abba rested his arm over my shoulder and lowered his voice. "Let me tell you something about gold, little one. It is best to have none at all. Once you begin to accumulate gold it makes your palm itch for more. Love of money is the root of all evil." He licked his lips. "So what have you brought for our supper?"

Other shepherds drifted in from the fields as I spread a cloth and sat out our meal. There was a large block of soft cheese with herbs kneaded in the way Abba preferred, fresh-baked barley loaves, parched grains in vinegar and oil with sliced cucumbers, dried fruits, eggs cooked hard in water and a skin of wine.

A man's voice from behind startled me. "Those apricots

look tasty."

A large hand reached over my shoulder into my open package of dried fruit and stole an apricot. I jerked around in surprise and watched the thief, my Uncle Chayim, grin as he popped the fruit into his mouth.

He and Abba looked enough alike that strangers sometimes confused them. Chayim was more than an uncle to me...almost a father. He called me his other daughter because I spent my earliest years in his household. Many of those evenings I crawled into my uncle's strong arms and fell asleep.

Chayim clapped my father on the back and dropped onto the grass beside him. "Twins, eh Ya'akov. An auspicious start to the lambing season." He grinned. "You may be ahead for now, brother, but this season is far from over. We shall see who wins out in the end."

"And how are you, little shepherdess?" He rummaged in his pack for supper as he spoke. "Tamar sent honey cakes. There may be enough to share, although you will have to fight me for them. I feel hungry as a lion tonight." He bared his teeth, gave a low growl, then chuckled deep in his belly.

Abba grabbed a stick from the pile of branches the younger boys gathered that afternoon and poked at the fire, sending sparks soaring into the sky. He continued prodding the embers until flames re-appeared, then tossed on several more logs. The circle around the fire filled as the other shepherds drifted in from the meadows. The men shared food and talked among themselves. I sat with my head down, listening as I ate.

Shemu'el sat opposite me, on the other side of the fire with his brothers and father. We stole glances at each other through the flames. He and his brothers talked and laughed, making me wonder what they said. Each time our eyes met he smiled. The fire painted a glow on his face and its light sparkled in his eyes.

* * *

The hungry lion shared Aunt Tamar's honey cakes like I knew he would. They left my fingers sticky so I walked down to a nearby creek to wash.

"May I come down?" Shemu'el asked from the top of the hill.

"Of course." The cold water made my hands tingle.

Shemu'el's footsteps drew closer then he plopped down beside me. "You do not mind me being here, do you?"

He understood that as the only maiden it was sometimes necessary for me to go away by myself.

"Oh no. Uncle Chayim brought honey cakes to share. I came to wash my sticky fingers."

He rubbed his hands together and grinned. "This is your first season with your own flock. You must be excited."

I beamed with pride. "Yes I am, thanks to you."

Shemu'el and his brothers each had their own sheep. He had been building his herd for several years in anticipation of the day he would take a wife.

"You give me too much credit, Rivkah. I did not rescue Liat. We drove the lion off together."

Shemu'el always said nice things that made me feel good inside. He never belittled me the way the other boys did. Stay and talk some more, my heart begged. Knowing the other boys would tease us if we were gone too long, I forced myself to say instead, "We should get back to the fire."

Shemu'el rose and extended an arm. His strong hand grasped mine and he pulled me up. He continued holding my hand as we walked back to the campfire. I imagined walking this way everywhere we went after we wed.

"As your herd increases you may want to introduce new bloodlines," Shemu'el said. "My brother Caleb has a fine new ram. He would let you use him if I asked for you. I watched the ram search out and mount some of our ewes; he is a very aggressive breeder."

My fingers quivered in his hand. "How nice. I...I will keep that in mind." Aggressive breeding was the last thing I wanted to discuss with Shemu'el.

Our eyes met in the moonlight.

Shemu'el noticed my embarrassment and let my fingers slip through his.

We walked the rest of the way in silence. Oh, how I hated that ram of Caleb's.

* * *

Abba and I rechecked the sheep before turning in. Like always, groups of shepherds kept watch in shifts while the others slept. If a predator appeared, or anything out of the ordinary occurred, they would rouse the others.

Those on the first watch left for the field and the rest of us took our places around the fire. The flames danced in the dark as the men began chanting *Ma'ariv*. I tugged my fleece cloak over me for a blanket and tucked it under my chin as they sang our evening prayers.

Using my arm as a pillow, I watched Shemu'el through the flames as he arranged his bedroll. I imagined us snuggled together and sleeping in each other's arms. Myriad stars spread across the heavens above me. An unseen weight pushed my eyelids closed and I drifted into a deep slumber.

~ 7 ~

*"And an angel of the Lord appeared to them, and the glory of the Lord shone around them, and they were filled with fear."*– Luke 2:9

"Look out! A star is falling on us."

I awoke with a start and squinted into the bright light racing toward us.

Abba hunched beside me staring into the sky. The terrified look on his face gave me a chill. What was happening? Nothing frightened Abba.

The light drew nearer, growing larger and larger, until it surrounded us. I scrunched between the other shepherds, making myself as small as possible. The other shepherds? What were the other shepherds doing clustered around me? When did they move to our side of the fire? What became of our watchmen? Why had no one sounded an alarm?

Too many questions and no answers.

Struck dumb with fright, we sat like statues, our faces turned to the sky. What at first appeared to be a falling star gradually took shape. The light came from the creature at the center of it. Placing a hand along my brow to shield my eyes, I squinted up at him. His light washed over us, pure and clear. Everything stilled as this powerful being hovered above us.

"Do not be afraid."

I cannot recall what his voice sounded like, or if he even had a voice. His words became a part of my thoughts without me knowing how. An incredible sense of peace washed over me, better even than waking from a nightmare in my father's arms.

The others felt it too. All around me people smiled and sighed in relief. We could breathe again; we had nothing to fear.

No matter what happened, we knew it would be good. Just four simple words. This mighty creature had said, *"Do not be afraid,"* and we cast away our fears as easily as one tossed aside their cloak at the end of the day.

We came to understand he was one of God's angels sent to bring us a message. I snuggled under Abba's left arm and stared into the sky. With my fears gone, I could now look up at the angel without squinting.

"I bring you good tidings of great joy, which shall be to all people," the angel said. "For unto you is born this day in the city of David a Savior. He is the *Mashiach*, the Lord. And this shall be a sign unto you; you shall find the babe wrapped in swaddling clothes and lying in a manger."

Then the night sky opened.

I gasped as more and more of these marvelous creatures poured out of the heavens as rapidly as barley kernels spill from a split sack. This heavenly host gathered about us, swirling above our heads, praising God and singing, "Glory to God in the highest, and on earth peace, good will toward men."

And then, as quickly as they appeared, they were gone. The sky closed around them and we were left in darkness, left staring up at the stars in wonder. The night never seemed darker than it did after the angels left.

"What was that light?"

"We have seen the *Shekinah*, the Cloud of Glory," Abba said. "The manifestation of the Most High God."

"And those creatures of light were his angels, cherubim or seraphim perhaps," Shemu'el added.

Shemu'el? How could I not have noticed him beside me?

Everyone grew quiet, thinking on this. All at once the men looked at one another and cried in a single voice, "Bethlehem. We must go to Bethlehem. Let us go and see this thing that has happened, which the Lord has told us about."

The men scurried about gathering their things and preparing for the trip.

"What about our sheep?" someone shouted. "Shepherds do not abandon their sheep. Have we forgotten there are ewes in the meadow about to give birth?"

The men stopped in their tracks and cast questioning glances at each other.

Yes, I thought, what of the sheep?

"We shall leave the sheep in the hands of the Lord," Abba said. "He would not have sent his messengers to call us if He did not expect us to go."

So off to Bethlehem we went.

* * *

When men are in a hurry they take long strides, making it difficult for people with short legs to keep up. The shepherds led the way and I ran alongside. Each time I stumbled in the dark Abba's strong arm caught me before I fell.

No one knew what to expect when we arrived in Bethlehem.

The angel gave us no directions, yet somehow we knew right where to go.

We turned the corner of Bethlehem's back streets and found a man sitting on the ground blocking the entrance to a stable. He had his coarse traveling cloak wrapped around himself as a blanket and his back propped against the post which framed the opening. He reminded me of a shepherd keeping watch in front of a sheepfold. Seeing his head resting on folded arms laid across his bent knees, I assumed he dozed.

As we drew nearer, he heard the scuffling of our footsteps and stirred. Pushing aside the cloak gathered about his face, he lifted his head and studied our little band warily.

He rose, stretched and rolled his shoulders before untying the straps of his *tefillin*. These small leather pouches contained verses from the Law. Jews tie them around their forehead and on their left arm near their heart in obedience to the Torah, which said, *"bind the commands, decrees and laws of the Lord to your forehead and to your heart."*

He had been praying, not sleeping.

The man stood and combed his fingers through the tangles of his beard, watching us as we approached. Though clearly tired, his dark, intelligent eyes remained alert. I knew just about everyone in Bethlehem, but not him. He must have come to be numbered in Caesar's census.

He held his large hands in front of him, not threatening, but prepared to defend if necessary. Defend what? What needed guarding in this little room attached to the back of a small house?

He moved to the center of the doorway. *"Shalom Aleichem.* Peace be unto you," he said. "What is it you seek?"

*"Aleichem Shalom.* Peace to you as well," Abba replied. "I am Ya'akov bar Yohan, a shepherd." Planting his staff in the soft dirt, he grabbed it with both hands and gently rocked from side to side as he spoke. "These are my friends and neighbors, other shepherds. We seek the one of whom the angels spoke."

The man's eyes widened. "Angels? I do not understand. I

know nothing of angels."

Abba and the other men all spoke at once, chattering in excited voices as they tried to explain what had happened in the fields. The bright light that surrounded us, the angelic being and the heavenly host singing, *"Peace on earth and goodwill to men."*

Then they told him about the message the angel gave us.

"We know only what we were told. The hand of the Most High urged us to leave our flocks and come to Bethlehem. We came without understanding why," the men confessed, spreading their arms in bewilderment. "Can you help us find this wondrous thing of which the angels spoke?"

"You have come to the right place," the man replied.

Recalling their fright when the heavens opened and the heavenly host poured out, the men shrank back. But as in the fields, their fears quickly gave way to excitement. Regaining their courage, they inched forward toward the doorway, stretching their necks and craning to see. His raised hand stopped them.

"You must wait here," he said, courteous but resolute. "The midwife and the other women just left. My wife is feeding her infant for the first time. They must not be disturbed." He smiled and motioned the men away from the entrance. "Come," he said, "we shall talk while we wait."

He seemed most interested in hearing about what happened to us in the fields.

"Tell me again all you saw and heard," he said, squatting. His eyes swept across the men circled around him. "Omit nothing."

He listened, interrupting to ask questions from time to time. Sometimes he made reference to one or another of the prophets. As Jewish men will do, the shepherds all replied at once, each giving their own interpretation, telling what this rabbi or that rabbi once said.

When they finished with the angels he asked about their new lambs. Were they healthy? Was the lamb crop good this year? He was a carpenter, he explained, from the North Country, from Nazareth in Galilee.

Laughing and nodding, the men discussed the kind of things men always talked about, tools and work.

Then, from inside the stable, a baby's cry pierced the quiet night.

~ **8** ~

*"And they went with haste and found Mary and Joseph, and the babe..."* —Luke 2:16

The lusty cry of the newborn echoed in the night air. The men paused, listened, then grinned and clapped the man on the back, congratulating him.

Everyone ignored me. Curious, I tiptoed away from the men and back to the entrance. And, since no one tried to stop me, I went inside. The family's animals had been tethered outside and the room, which usually housed them, had been cleaned and prepared for these travelers.

A young woman sat on a blanket laid over a bed of fresh straw near the back of the stable. Head down, she concentrated on moving her newborn from one side to the other. Adjusting the child in her arms, she tugged her cloak open and exposed her other breast. She brushed his cheek and he latched on, eating as greedily as a newborn lamb.

Watching her made me smile.

When he finished, she rested him on her lap and adjusted her clothing. She patted his back until he burped and then nestled him against her bosom.

I crept forward into the circle of light surrounding them.

Her head jerked up. My crinkling sound of my footsteps on the straw must have startled her.

I lowered my eyes, waiting for some signal she was not upset with me for being there.

"Hello. Who are you?" She lifted a finger and motioned me

closer.

"My name is Rivkah. *Shalom Aleichem.*"

"And to you." She smiled. "I am Miryam. That was Yosef, my husband, at the doorway."

"The baby's father."

For an instant an unsettled look clouded Miryam's face. She didn't seem to know how to answer me.

She chewed her lip as she thought. Then a load seemed to lift off her shoulders. "Yes," she nodded, "Yosef will be the child's father."

"How are you feeling?" I asked, noting the fatigue in her eyes.

"Tired," she said. "Tired, but very, very happy."

She eased the blanket back and let me see the baby's face. It looked pink and slightly wrinkled, pretty much like every other new baby I'd seen. I reached out and brushed back a few stray hairs from the child's forehead.

Miryam seemed pleased.

New mothers enjoy having people fuss over their babies. Every time I see a baby I always try to act like they are extra special. Even the ugly ones. Not that this child was ugly; it was the sweetest baby I had ever seen.

"May I hold your baby?"

My request shocked her. New mothers are always nervous about letting people hold their babies. Some sheep are the same way. They get very protective when they have their first lamb and try to butt you if you come too close. But, just like the ewes, new mothers eventually get better. Time passes and they worry less.

"Will you be very careful?"

A part of me wanted to tell her I knew all about newborns. I had handled more baby lambs than you could ever count. Pulled them out when they got stuck, held them up to their mother's teat if they were too weak to nurse and cut the cord for ewes too weak to do it themselves. Many a cold night a new lamb slept with me nestled inside my cloak.

Of course there were also the babies of the shepherd's wives. My younger cousins, Aunt Tamar's children, needed my help every day. But Miryam was new at this, so I thought it best to humor her.

I sat down and scooted back until we touched. Then she reached around and placed the infant in my arms. The first thing I did was loosen the wrap and peek in to check. The angels were right; it was a boy. When I glanced back over my shoulder, our eyes met and we shared a smile.

Every mother wants her firstborn to be a boy. It pleases her husband. By Jewish law the first boy child belongs to the Temple. Yosef and Miryam would have to go to Jerusalem and make an offering to ransom him back.

I re-wrapped the swaddling and leaned forward, putting my mouth very close to his little ear, and whispered, "*Sh'ma Yisrael Adonai eleheinu Adonai ehad.*"

She liked seeing me do that.

The Sh'ma is the first prayer of every Jew: *Hear O Israel, the Lord is our God; the Lord is one.*

He squirmed and made a whimpering sound in his sleep. Thinking he was uncomfortable, I adjusted him in my arms.

Miryam reached around me and put her arms under mine to help support him. "Here," she said, "let me help you."

Imagine. She worried about me dropping her baby. It was easy to see how she might think that, but given a little time she would learn.

Together, we rocked from side to side. He snuggled against me and I sang the Jewish lullaby, *Lailah Tov Motek*, Goodnight, my darling. His little lips made sucking motions as he dozed.

Shuffling footsteps and whispered voices came from the front of the stable. The men had finally come to see the baby. Yosef and Abba were in the lead. When they saw me sitting with Miryam holding the baby, they came to a halt. The surprised look on their faces made me grin.

* * *

Eight days later, when Yosef circumcised him, they named their baby Yeshua. Since they had to make trips to the Temple to ransom their son and then again for Miryam's purification, they remained in Bethlehem. They may have intended to return to Galilee, but one thing led to another and they ended up staying on.

At first they knew very few people, so each time Abba made a trip to Bethlehem I tagged along. He would drop me off at Yosef's carpenter shop to visit with Miryam and Yeshua while he conducted his business.

Times were becoming hard for Abba and me. We paid taxes and duties and road tolls to Herod each time we took sheep to Jerusalem, plus the poll tax, the annual Temple tax, first tithes and second tithes. We paid and paid until Abba's purse was nearly empty.

Raising more lambs seemed to be the answer. One Shabbat we asked Uncle Chayim to watch our flock so we could go to the synagogue in Bethlehem to pray about it. Red streaks filled the eastern sky when we left the house. We talked and sang Psalms along the way.

Some people at the synagogue gave us unkind looks and whispered comments about smelly shepherds when we arrived. You might expect that in Jerusalem, but not in a farming town like Bethlehem.

Many of the people in Jerusalem lived very well. They grew proud and looked down on shepherds and country folk. Annas, the former high priest, and his family lived in homes made of cut block, each stone polished until it sparkled. Their lavish homes crowded the hills west of the Temple.

I sometimes saw children of the rich when we delivered lambs to the Temple. A rich man's daughter had little in common with me. They wore the finest linen, gold bracelets and anklets and jeweled earrings.

Even girls my age colored their eyelids and cheeks and

perfumed their hair. And they never sweat. Why should they? They had slaves to do all their work. In the summer, some of them even had a slave trailing behind them carrying a sunshade.

I had lived with this prejudice all my life. When you are a shepherd, you get used to people not giving you any respect. The scribes and the Pharisees murmur we shepherds do not keep all the rules of the Law. Well, perhaps not down to the last iota and dot.

We were shepherds, not Pharisees, after all. We did the best we could. When I was alone at night with the flock under the stars, I felt as close to God as any High Priest ever did in the Holy of Holies.

Yosef and Miryam were at the synagogue when we arrived. I squeezed in beside Miryam in the women's section, wishing her "Shabbat Shalom."

I got to hold my little friend, Yeshua. He brought the toy sheep I made for him. I cut a scrap of fleece, sewed it and stuffed it with barley husks.

He shook it and said, "Baa, baa, baa."

I pretended to be upset and tried to shush him, but I secretly enjoyed it.

A few weeks earlier I found a burl on a branch that Abba pruned from one of our olive trees. While Shemu'el worked on his bowls I whittled at my burl, squaring the sides and putting a point at the bottom. It would become a *dreidel*.

After I smoothed it, I planned to ask Shemu'el to carve the letters *nun, gimmel, hay* and *shin* on it. One letter on each of its four sides. They stand for nes gadol hayah sham—A great miracle happened here. When my *driedel*'s finished, I'll rub it with some of Shemu'el's almond oil and beeswax finish. I plan to give it to Yeshau the next time we go to Bethlehem and teach him how to make it spin.

\* \* \*

Abba made a special mark on the left ear of all the twin ewe lambs. When he decided which to sell and which to keep, he selected the keepers from among the twins. He believed that a twin, when bred, was more likely to produce more twins.

At the synagogue I asked the Lord to bless our flock and let every ewe bring forth two lambs this spring so we would have enough money to pay our taxes. After our visit to Bethlehem life continued in a normal manner for a time, then strange things began happening.

~ **9** ~

*"Rise, take the child and his mother, and flee to Egypt,..."*—Matthew 2:13

A few weeks after we went to Bethlehem the first ewes began dropping their lambs. Perhaps the Lord answered my prayer. It felt like we were getting more twins than usual. Not all twins, though. Maybe I asked for more than we deserved.

It was the middle of *Shebat*, the month of spring lambing and we spent our nights in the fields, looking after the sheep from a watchtower. Being up high gave us a bird's eye view of the field. We could spot predators long before they threatened our flock. Constructed of mortar and stones gathered from the surrounding fields, these round towers had a lot in common with our house. Both of them had an outside stairway leading to the top. It was flat, like our roof, and they each had a low wall around them so no one fell over the side.

I stretched to my full height and pointed north. "Look."

Together Abba and I watched the far-off silhouette of a solitary wayfarer trudging toward us on the south road. I rubbed my eyes and squinted at the dark image. A man led a donkey piled high with...well, he was too far away to say.

It surprised me to see a lone traveler. Long strings of camels often slipped past in the moonlight while we tended our sheep. Merchant caravans preferred traveling at night when it was cool, but few others dared be on the road after sunset. Even pilgrims traveled during the day and in the company of friends or relatives. Bandits lurked in the Judean hills ready to pounce on the unwary.

A full moon hung low in the heavens, shimmering across the surrounding fields. The sheep gathered in tight clusters along the grassy hillside below us. They shone white in the moonlight, reminding me of the limestone boulders strewn along the road to Jerusalem.

The high-pitched, cackling laughter of a hyena reverberated in the darkness.

Jerking up, I cocked my head and listened. An eerie stillness settled over the valley, a tense waiting.

Abba tossed his cloak aside.

My heart thumped. I leaned forward and scanned the brush for movement. What else might be out there? Even after two years, I had not forgotten the day Shemu'el and I drove off the lion.

The sheep stirred on the hillside below us.

Abba pulled his *shebet* from his sash. The knurled piece of ancient grapewood bore the stains of many a predator's blood. He rocked it in his hand as he counted the shadowy shapes scattered across the dark meadow.

Everyone accounted for. He gave a relieved sigh.

Most ewes go off by themselves when the time comes to deliver their lambs. A missing sheep often meant someone was giving birth. We had to track them down right away because she could be in distress and need our help. Jackals, wolves and hyenas became more aggressive during lambing season. They often stalked isolated ewes, waiting to steal their newborn lambs.

Abba left to soothe the sheep.

I rechecked the road. The man leading the donkey had gotten closer. What I imagined to be his pack of goods turned out to be a passenger, a woman. He took quick, measured steps, checking the moonlit road in front of him then casting furtive glances over his shoulder.

When Abba returned I pointed out the man's odd behavior. "He looks like he is running away from something. Do you think he is being chased?"

The man led the donkey around a curve in the road and headed straight at us. He spent so much time checking the road behind that he failed to notice us watching from the tower. Moonlight flooded down on him. His distorted shadow, overly tall and stretched-out looking, moved along the grass with each step he and the donkey took.

My heart leaped in my chest. I recognized them! It was Miryam on the donkey and her husband, Yosef, leading it. They should be asleep in their bed behind his carpentry shop in Bethlehem. What were they doing out here all by themselves so late at night?

"Look, Abba. It's my friends, Miryam and Yosef. Can I say hello to them?"

"I suppose it would be all right."

I skipped down the stairway and began pulling up handfuls of grass.

"What are you doing?" Abba asked.

I stooped for another handful. "Gathering grass for Isaias, Yosef's donkey."

"Yosef named his donkey, Isaias?"

"No. I did." Why explain about the jokes I played on Yosef by giving his donkey a different name each time I visited? I ran toward the road waving my grass and hollering, "Miryam, Yosef, stop. It is me, Rivkah."

Yosef made an unpleasant face when he saw me. He pulled back on the donkey's rope, bringing the little animal to a halt. Miryam whispered something to him and Yosef's shoulders relaxed.

"Hello, Isaias," I said to the donkey. I still could not believe they were so far from home. "What are you doing out this night?"

I scratched the donkey's long nose and fed him clumps of

fresh grass. He seemed happy to see me even if no one else was. Isaias raised his sad, brown eyes and stared at me as if to say, "It was not my idea to be out late at night. I was happy sleeping in my stall until Yosef roused me."

In back, Yosef muttered to himself while he checked the baggage. He came around the side of the donkey shaking his head.

"Why must you always call him names? The poor creature has a weak enough intellect without you changing his name every week or two. It confuses him. And calling an animal by the name of so great a prophet is disrespectful."

I grinned up at him. "Maybe I will call him Caesar Augustus instead." The donkey took another mouthful of grass. "Or perhaps, King Herod."

"You are a foolish little girl. If a soldier heard you say such a thing, he would knock you down and kick you across the street."

It was not like him to be short with me.

"It was only a jest. I meant nothing by it." Lowering my head, I offered the donkey the last of my grass. "Here, nameless donkey." I dabbed at my eyes and scratched the donkey's nose while he chewed.

"She meant no disrespect," Miryam whispered.

Yosef's mouth formed a tight line. "I am sorry, Rivkah. I did not mean to upset you. We are in a great hurry and must not be delayed."

The bundle on Miryam's back began wiggling and making noises. She gave Yosef a loving look. "You have had little sleep today, husband, and you are tired. Rest here while I feed the baby. We have a long night ahead of us."

He gave a resigned nod. Giving the rope a sharp tug, Yosef led the donkey over to the side of road.

Abba appeared over the brow of the hill. His eyes went from me, to Miryam, to the man leading the animal.

"*Shalom Aleichem*, Yosef. You appear to be a man full of

troubling thoughts. Is all well with you this evening?"

Motioning Abba aside, Yosef stepped away from the donkey. They turned their backs to me and conversed in hushed whispers. Whatever it was that upset Yosef, he did not want me to know about it.

I walked around to the side of the donkey, looked up, and smiled. "*Shalom Aleichem*, Miryam."

"*Aleichem Shalom*, Rivkah. Ignore Yosef. He thinks of other things tonight." She glanced back over her shoulder, studying the moon. "And how are you this night?"

"Abba and I are watching the sheep. Lambing time again." I rested my hands on my hips and gave her a stern look. "Do you know how dangerous it is to travel alone at night?"

Miryam chuckled. "Sometimes, my young friend, a person must do what they must do. Fear not, God is with us. Yosef plans to join a caravan along the way. If not in Hebron, then surely by the time we reach Beersheba."

"Beersheba? Why are you going to Beersheba?"

She nibbled at her lip. Miryam's eyes flicked to Yosef, still in deep conversation with Abba, then back to me. She shook her head. Her expression said she could tell no more.

"Did I wake Yeshua?"

"Oh, no." She loosened the strap and swung the cloth bundle on her back around to her lap. "He has been awake for a little while now making hungry noises." She folded back his blanket. "Would you take him for a moment?"

She handed him down to me. At eighteen months, Yeshua was much heavier than the first time I held him. Miryam no longer worried because Yeshua and I played so often at their home behind Yosef's shop.

Miryam slipped off the donkey's back and onto the grass. As she stretched, her eyes searched the moonlit road a second time. She made no attempt to mask her concerns.

The men squatted by the side of the road whispering and

scratching lines in the dirt.

"We have heavy cloaks in the watchtower."

At the sound of my voice, Yeshua blinked up at me with a toothy grin. I lifted him up to my shoulder and kissed him on the cheek. He hugged my neck and said, "Rivvy," the way my little cousin, Yohan, used to.

I sat on my cloak and offered Abba's to Miryam. Yeshua and I played grab my finger while she loosened her clothing. I sat beside her, listening to her hum *Lailah Tov Motek* as he nursed.

"I wish I had a baby like Yeshua to feed and care for."

Miryam smiled. "I remember watching women nurse their babies when I was a girl and thinking the same thing. Your womanhood will come upon you before you know it. Then a young man will knock at the door asking your father if he can take you for his wife."

"I already know who it will be."

She arched an eyebrow. "Do you now?"

"A shepherd boy in our village and he is very handsome. His name is Shemu'el."

"I am sure he is."

"And he is strong and brave and brings me presents."

She paused, trying to decide what to say next. "Rivkah, you and I both know the marriage arrangements are made by the men in the family."

"No matter. Shemu'el will be the one."

"And you know this how?" She switched Yeshua to her other arm and closed her cloak over him.

"Because I love him. Better a meal of vegetables where there is love than a fatted calf with hatred."

"Time will tell, my young friend. Time will tell."

"But marriages are *b'shert*. If something is destined by the will of God, it must come to pass."

"True enough." Miryam hugged me tightly and kissed my

forehead. "Keep in mind, God's ways are not our ways. In addition to happiness, God's plan sometimes brings heartache and sacrifice."

~ 10 ~

*"And being warned in a dream not to return to Herod, they departed to their own country by another way."* —Matthew 2:12

I held Yeshua while Miryam settled herself on the donkey. He grinned up at me sleepy eyed. Putting my mouth close to his little ear, I whispered the Birkat Kohanim. This priestly blessing was repeated many times each day in the Temple, "May the Lord bless and keep you. May the Lord cause his countenance to shine upon you and be gracious unto you. May the Lord favor you and grant you peace."

"May it be his will. Blessed be the Lord God, the God of Israel, from everlasting to everlasting," Miryam responded for her young son.

I kissed him. "Good-bye Yeshua. Be safe while we are apart, *Yeki'ri.*"

When we first began playing together I called Yeshua my little king. After all, the angel told us he would be the *Mashiach*. Miryam heard me do this and asked me not to. She said Yeshua would find his destiny in his own way and time. From then on I called him *Yeki'ri*, my precious one.

I dug in my bag and offered her the *dreidel* I had carved. "Here. I made this for Yeshua. I planned to give it to him the next time I visited."

She thanked me and tucked it away in a saddlebag. Then she said something that sent a chill up my spine. "It will be good for him to have something that reminds him of home."

"Home? Where are you going? When will we see each other again?"

Some questions, it seems, get no answer. Miryam adjusted

the slumbering babe on her back and nodded her readiness to Yosef. As the donkey plodded away, she waved. "All in God's good time, Rivkah. *Kol Tuv*, my little friend."

I returned her wish to Be Well with a heavy heart. They grew smaller and smaller until they became a speck on the horizon. I leaned into Abba and he rested his hands upon my shoulders.

"Where are they going?"

"For Yeshua's sake, it is better that you not know."

"I do not understand."

He dropped to one knee and held me by my arms. "Yosef has been warned. The child is no longer safe in Bethlehem."

I looked at him with questioning eyes.

He shook his head. "I can tell you no more, my little dove. In time, perhaps things will become clear. For now, know this, you must forget you ever saw them. Say nothing of this night to anyone."

Though it made no sense at the time, as a good daughter I would do what my father asked.

He took my hand. "Come, time to check the ewes."

\* \* \*

Hours later the sound of many hooves roused me. I snapped awake in an instant, my heart pounding. It was dark and cold, the bone-chilling cold which came just before dawn. My cloak was damp, heavy with dew.

"Listen, Abba. Horses," I whispered. "Many horses, coming toward us."

He grabbed his rod from where it rested against the tower's low wall. "Stay here. I will see who it is."

"No. I want to go with you." I jerked my little rod out of my sash and rose, ready to fight.

He opened his mouth to speak, but shook his head and gave an angry grunt instead.

I followed one step behind. By the time we reached the roadway an entire cavalry had drawn into a line in front of us.

Never had I seen such finery. They looked like a royal escort. The war horses, one indistinguishable from the next, were black as night, sleek, broad-chested and muscular. Their harnesses, bridles and saddles gleamed with silver buckles and trim. Even their saddle blankets matched, deep blue with a white star at one corner. These massive stallions tossed their heads and pawed the ground, blowing and snorting.

Each of the riders wore a plumed helmet and a blue cape drawn around pure white tunics. Their heavy leather breeches extended to their ankles and an armored coat of silver scales protected their upper body. They carried a sword on their right side, holstered in a heavy scabbard, and a javelin slung along the horse's flank. A hammered shield, emblazoned with gold lions and eagles, hung from the left side of each saddle.

Farther down the road a group of pack camels plodded toward us. Three riders pushed through the formation of horses and reined their mounts to a stop. A uniformed man leaped off his horse and gathered the leads as the three men dismounted.

Instead of a soldier's uniform and armor, all three wore rich brocades and silks. Their tunics were long and loose, with gold tassels around the hem. Their purple cloaks were as beautiful as those worn by the High Priest. Elaborate turbans, each secured with a jewel, encircled their heads.

Our shepherd's rods were of no use against such an overwhelming force. Abba sank to his knees and bowed low. I dropped down beside him, quaking.

"Arise. You have nothing to fear from us," their leader said in heavily accented Aramaic. "We are on a mission of peace and diplomacy."

The man was tall and thin with bushy white eyebrows above his welcoming eyes. He towered above his two companions. I stared up at his gaunt, deeply-lined face as I rose and smoothed my tunic.

"Are you kings?" I asked.

He stroked his white beard and gave me a benevolent smile. "No, my child, we are not kings." He turned to Abba. "Pardon my rudeness. I am Melchior." He swept his arm in the direction of the others. "My companions...Gaspar and Balthazar. In our country they call us *Magoi*, the Great Ones of the Upper House of the Megistanes. We are advisors to Phraates, ruler of the Parthian Dynasty."

The man called Gaspar studied us for a moment. "You are Jews, yes?"

Abba seemed to stand taller as he replied, "We are shepherds, children of Avraham who worship the one and only God of the universe."

"We came to your king bearing gifts," Balthazar said.

"You have seen Herod?"

"Indeed. We paid a courtesy call to Herod, the Idumean pretender." Melchior spat on the ground. "With his army away on maneuvers, he tolerated our presence and feigned hospitality. We expected little more. After all, forty years ago it was the Parthians who killed his brother, Phasaelus, drove Herod from this land, and restored Hasmonean rule. The only thing Herod hates more than Parthians is the thought of a rival to his throne. We found the king we sought, the true King of the Jews, in Bethlehem, not Jerusalem."

"Did angels tell you where to find him?"

"Angels?" Melchior chuckled and shook his head. "No, my child. Not angels, prophets."

"Prophets?"

"Your prophet Daniy'yel, the man Nebuchadnezzar re-named, Belteshazzar. He once held a position in the court of Babylon and is still revered by my people. His scrolls and others like it have a place of honor in the Royal Library. They foretell the birth of a King who will be your *Mashiach*, the Rock not cut by human hands. Our mathematicians calculated the dates and predicted his birth. Our astrologers studied the night skies." He pointed into the dark, pre-dawn sky. "We followed a star that led us to the babe."

I danced with excitement. He meant Yeshua. They had been to see my little king. "Abba! Abba, does he know—"

My father clamped his large hand over my mouth.

Melchior gave him a reassuring smile. "Do not worry about her unwittingly betraying confidences, my friend. We, too, have been warned."

My father's eyes sent the old man a message and he said no more.

All these secrets were getting worrisome.

Melchior dropped to one knee and took my hand. "You wonder why we have come, and I will tell you. There are still many of your people in our Empire, descendants of Jews who, many hundreds of years ago, chose to remain in Babylon rather than return to Jerusalem."

He lifted his eyes and gazed far off. "We are on a diplomatic mission. Someday this King, this *Mashiach* of yours, will crush all the kingdoms of this world. He will conquer not with war, but with peace and love. When he does, he will find allies among the Parthians."

"How may we serve you?" Abba asked.

"We planned to take on water and provisions at Jerusalem before heading east from whence we came. Our plans have changed. We will not be going to your holy city. Still, we must replenish our waterskins and allow our animals to drink their fill."

"My daughter will lead your men to water."

Melchior stepped aside and conferred with one of his chiefs for a moment. The man turned, barked a command in a strange language and the soldiers dismounted as a group.

As they formed into a line, Melchior said, "The Parthians and the Romans maintain an uneasy peace sustained by mutual distrust and our cavalry's consistent ability to outflank their legions. We wish to draw as little attention to ourselves as possible. Despite our worthy mission, Caesar would not appreciate so deep an incursion into his territory."

The chief of the guard snapped to attention in front of me. "We await your command," he said with a bow.

Turning, I pointed the way.

A long line of men, horses and camels stretched out behind me as I led them down the trail to the lake where we watered our sheep. Leaving them there, I traipsed back up the hill. The first rays of daylight were breaking over the peaks of the Judean Mountains.

Abba knelt beside the road with a soldier at his side. Melchior, Gaspar and Balthazar bent over with hands resting on their knees and looked over his shoulder while Abba scratched a map in the dirt.

He pointed in the direction of the rising sun. "Due east of here, on the other side of those mountains, is Lake Asphaltitis." His stick skipped over the long row of upturned points representing the Judean mountains and came down in the center of a large oblong shape.

"Do not go there. Its waters are dead. Neither man nor beast can drink of them. Pillars of pure salt rise from its depths." He raised his eyes to the man at his side.

The man nodded in understanding.

"To the south of us is Herodium, one of Herod's retreats. Here." The point of his stick poked into the dust, marking it. "It has a small garrison of troops." He moved the stick closer to Jerusalem and poked again, this time into one of his peaks. "Hyrcania, a Jewish city in the mountains. Best to thread your way between them. Here is the pass," he said, tracing a squiggly line between the peaks.

"Can a camel train make it through?"

"Some of the defiles are narrow, but they can advance single file. It is safe; there are no troops anywhere near there. This route will bring you out near the top of Lake Asphaltitis. Follow the shoreline north past Secacah, a peaceful community of the Essenes — devout Jews who spend their days in prayer and meditation. Beyond Secacah you will encounter the sweet water of the Jordan River. Perea lies east of the river, Nabatea to the south and The Decapolis to the north."

"We can retrace our steps from there," the soldier said.

He retrieved a quill and inkhorn from his saddlebag and copied the drawing onto a scroll. When he finished, he handed it to my father for his approval. They rose smiling and dusted their knees.

"For your trouble," Melchior said. The gold coins he placed in Abba's palm sparkled in the morning sun.

My father contemplated them for a moment then shook his head. "Thank you for your generosity, but no. Our Law demands we provide hospitality and assistance to the sojourner. I have done nothing to merit payment and we are not beggars."

"As you wish." Melchior returned the coins to his bag and said something in another language. A camel driver rummaged in one of his packs. He returned with a large, square package wrapped in a type of papyrus and tied with twine. Melchior removed a sword from one of the men's scabbards and sliced the twine.

Motioning me forward, he leaned down and handed it to me. Inside was the biggest block of Persian candy I had ever seen.

\* \* \* \* \*

Read the bestselling story of Rivkah, Shemu'el, their family and friends. WITNESS is available at Amazon.com in both print and digital format for the Kindle.

*The Saga of the Early Church Continues—*
# DISCIPLE
Book Two of The Seeds of Christianity™ Series
*The Seeds find Fertile Soil*

Rivkah and her family convert to the Way of Yeshua. Then Temple authorities refuse to buy lambs from Yeshua's followers. Unable to survive in their home settlement, they move to Jerusalem where they encounter Saul of Tarsus, the scourge of the early Church...and Stephen, the first to die for his faith. Increasing persecution forces them out again. Leaving Jerusalem, they head for Antioch with Simon Peter to establish the Church there.

Experience life in the early Church where the first Christians struggle to live out the teachings of Yeshua in an often hostile environment. Sit beside the twelve apostles as they partition the world and begin their mission of preaching and teaching.

Stand beside Channah as she watches a mob stone the man she loves. Meet Pavlos of Antioch, the mute giant whose actions speak louder than words, and whose innate goodness births a ministry to the weak and helpless. Weep with Eleana, the young Parthian woman who was savagely attacked by a Roman soldier and must now decide whether to bear the child that must be his.

*The Church at Antioch Comes into Its Own—*

# APOSTLE

Book Three of The Seeds of Christianity™ Series

Follow the lives of Rivkah and Shemu'el as they continue to spread the good news in Antioch and beyond. Tensions surface as the number of non-Jewish converts rises in Antioch. Barnabus goes to Tarsus and returns with Paul. Though some oppose his new role in the Church, Paul leaves on his first missionary journey accompanied by Barnabus and Yohan Markus.

This tale of the Early Church takes a troubling turn when Rivkah's youngest son, Yudah. adopts a pagan lifestyle and Antioch trembles in the grip of a ruthless serial killer. While Pavlos roams the streets looking for the murderer, Shemu'el fears he already knows the killer's identity.

The beloved disciple, Yohan, has relocated to Ephesus for Miryam's protection. He brings Shemu'el a new convert named Ignatius and asks him to mentor the young man. Though surrounded by chaos, the church in Antioch prospers, growing in size and influence as the Apostles take the message to the world.

*The Emperor is Dead. Long Live the Emperor!*

# MARTYR

Book Four of The Seeds of Christianity™ Series

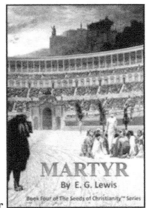

Simon Peter calls Rivkah and Shemu'el from Antioch to Rome. And, in a strange convergence of events, Rivkah's son, Yudah, meets Rhebekka, the girl of his dreams on Cyprus. Meanwhile, in Rome, Nero now wears the crown and Paul arrives in chains as a prisoner.

Rivkah and her family narrowly escape the huge conflagration that leaves most of Rome in ashes. Angry voices rise in the street accusing the Emperor Nero of being the incendiary and he desperately searches for a scapegoat to divert attention. His wife Poppaea, suggests he blame the Christians. She realizes too late that like Pandora, she has unleashed a demon that no one can ever control.

The Christians construct the first catacomb and its niches quickly fill as more and more believers are slain for their faith. As the numbers climb, Shemu'el realizes they have a traitor in their midst. But how can he identify this false Christian who's selling out his friends to save his own skin?

*Don't miss the emotional climax to*

*The Seeds of Christianity*™

Made in the USA
Middletown, DE
02 October 2024

61817901R00080